HATS BY MADAME

Paulette

HATS BY MADAME

Paulette

Paris Milliner Extraordinaire

Annie Schneider

Foreword by Stephen Jones

141 illustrations, 35 in color

Thames & Hudson

To Jacques

The author and publisher would like to thank Patrick Mauriès most warmly for his
contribution to this project from its conception.

Page 2: Asymmetric shell-shaped cap in velvet, 1950.

Hats by Madame Paulette © 2014 Thames & Hudson Ltd, London
Text © 2014 Annie Schneider
Foreword © 2014 Stephen Jones

First published in 2014 in hardcover in the United States of America by Thames & Hudson Inc.,
500 Fifth Avenue, New York, New York 10110

thamesandhudsonusa.com

Library of Congress Catalog Card Number 2013948280

ISBN 978-0-500-51731-4

Printed and bound in China by C & C Offset Printing Co. Ltd

Contents

Foreword – Stephen Jones 8

'Queen among Milliners' 12

Part 1

1 The Early Years 18

2 Starting Off 24

3 The 1940s 30

4 Postwar Celebrity 46

Part 2

5 Famous Fittings 62

6 America Comes Calling 74

7 High Society 78

8 America Again 96

9 Stage and Screen 102

10 With Cecil Beaton 108

Part 3

11 By Appointment 118

12 End of an Era 136

13 The Couture Houses 150

Acknowledgments 157

Further Reading 158

Illustration Credits 159

Index 160

Above: Paulette in her Paris salon, c. 1948.
Photograph by Willy Maywald.

Previous pages: Madame Paulette in her
workshop, 1973.

Foreword
Stephen Jones

How that name sends shivers down my spine! In 1986 the writer Patrick Cabasset, now fashion editor-in-chief of *L'Officiel*, wrote an article entitled 'Stephen Jones, la nouvelle Madame Paulette' and I have been trying to live up to it ever since.

I never actually met Paulette, but mutual friends have satisfied my curiosity with a glint in their eyes. Béatrice Paul regaled me with stories of how they worked and gossiped late into the night creating marvels for the Claude Montana fashion show extravaganzas of the early 1980s. Monsieur Ré, Paulette's block-maker, told me with a wry smile how precise yet charming she was, sitting in the corner of his atelier making sure her blocks were perfect and completed before her competitors. Chuckling with anecdotes, one of her favourite milliners Josiane (who in later life worked in my atelier at Christian Dior) demonstrated how to make a signature Paulette turban.

The turban, her fabulous wartime invention encapsulating French coquetry combined with American glamour, is how she is best remembered by milliners and fashion historians around the world.

Yet this wonderful new book shows the breadth of her oeuvre, from virtuoso elegance for Princess Grace of Monaco to hyper-fantasies for Thierry Mugler.

The Design: amazing! The Technique: impeccable! The Clients: wow! The confidence, the chic, the style. Everything about her world seems extraordinary, from the hundreds of milliners in her workrooms to her tours of American department stores.

Of course, in this day and age, hats do not enjoy the status and importance that they once did. That role is fulfilled by handbags, but nothing else is quite as evocative of time and place as a hat, nothing as striking and, crucially, nothing as personal. Even now in the twenty-first century when a fashion designer wants to evoke a particular spirit, be it vintage, contemporary or futuristic, headgear is involved. Whether dressed down in a grungy beanie for a chilly Monday morning in November or dressed up in a formal pink straw for Royal Ascot in June, the hat is the key to the look. A hat is still such a powerful talisman, although Paulette did say in an interview with *Harper's Bazaar* in 1984: 'I am shocked today by the lack of elegant millinery: the madder the hat, the better. If not, wear a scarf!'

From this you would be right in thinking that Paulette was feisty and opinionated, but I know that she was also generous and kind. In the 1970s she took Catherine Rivière, who is now directrice of haute couture at Dior, under her wing and showered her with retro skull-fitting turbans; one particular jersey number was featured in the exhibition 'Hats: An Anthology by Stephen Jones' at London's Victoria and Albert Museum in 2009.

And her legacy? She is the Queen of French millinery. While other hallowed milliners such as Reboux, Svend or Albouy have faded into obscurity, Paulette still shines as the most influential of her generation. Why is this? Possibly because she will be always be remembered for evoking the 'Resistance Fashion' of the Second World War, but she was also the last of the generation of great French milliners who stitched *savoir faire* into each seam, steamed seduction into their sweeping veils and made every feather tremble with chic *à la Parisienne*.

Chapeau Paulette!

'Queen among Milliners'

Elegant, imaginative and witty, Pauline de la Bruyère, known as Paulette, was dubbed 'queen among milliners and milliner to queens'. Nowadays people barely recall the importance of hats, let alone the role of milliners in the first half of the twentieth century, yet Paulette employed more than a hundred women in her workrooms on Avenue Franklin D. Roosevelt in Paris, and opened shops in Buenos Aires, London and New York.

Paulette's fame was international. Over the years, monarchs, wives of heads of state, women from high society and the *haute bourgeoisie*, along with numerous actresses, all ordered hats by the dozen for the events that shaped their fashionable lifestyles: dinners, races at Longchamp, private views, cocktails, suppers and balls.

Greta Garbo, Marlene Dietrich, Gloria Swanson, Rose Kennedy, Eva Perón, the Begum Aga Khan III, Queen Soraya of Afghanistan, Rita Hayworth, Princess Paola of Belgium, Princess Grace of Monaco,

Paulette, 1946.
Photograph by Harcourt.

Claude Pompidou and the Duchess of Windsor could all rub shoulders with – or carefully avoid – one another in her salons.

As if that were not enough, Paulette also made hats for several fashion houses, either anonymously or under her own label, and presented her own collections twice a year.

After launching the famous '*turban-bicyclette*', her first major achievement, she continued to invent extraordinary, flattering and audacious headdresses that enhanced the beauty of the women who wore them.

From the 1940s until the 1980s, great fashion photographers such as Horst P. Horst, Henry Clarke, Richard Avedon, Helmut Newton, William Klein and Guy Bourdin fought over her toques, capelines (hats with soft, wide brims), boaters, pillboxes and evening caps for *Vogue* and *Harper's Bazaar*. Paulette also had a particular passion for headdresses for the theatre and cinema, a passion born out of her collaborations with Christian Bérard, Jean Cocteau and Cecil Beaton. She worked with Bérard on his poetic creations for *Amphitryon* and *Don Juan*. In collaboration with Beaton, she produced the amazing hats worn by Audrey Hepburn in *My Fair Lady*, as well as hats for *Gigi* and *An Ideal Husband*.

Such projects both delighted her and allowed her to express her inexhaustible imagination.

Indefatigable, she was still coming up with astonishingly modern hats for Thierry Mugler and Claude Montana at the age of eighty-four.

Paulette's unique personality, style, humour, creativity and gift of absolute elegance counted for much in the world of fashion, and she continues to influence designers to this day.

Her artistic sense was based on unfailing technique, a rigorous approach, and a sense of balance and lightness, all of which combined to make her hats inimitable, thus accounting for her clients' faithfulness and her long career.

How does someone become a milliner, not to mention the most famous milliner of their time, without the relevant education? This is one of the questions that this book will attempt to answer, a task as inspiring as it is difficult since Paulette did not have an explanation herself: 'No matter how far back into my childhood I go,' she confessed, 'I can't find any hint of a premonition about my chosen career. My artistic gifts were limited to drawing caricatures of my teachers.' Too modest or unaware of her real gifts and her talent for creativity, as we shall see in the following pages, Paulette

was one of the most important figures in twentieth-century fashion, despite the fact that her specialism was the apparently unassuming yet nevertheless essential area of accessories. 'Little nothings', as we know, are the true signatures of style.

Dorian Leigh, hat by Paulette, Paris, 1949.
Photograph by Richard Avedon.

The Early Years

1

Pauline Adam was born in 1900 in a large apartment in the Plaine-Monceau district of Paris. Her mother died in childbirth. Together with her two older brothers, she was brought up by her father, one of the directors of the chocolate factory Reine Wilhelmine, and her maternal grandfather, who resembled a character from a novel. He had made his fortune manufacturing tennis racquets, and croquet and boules equipment, and he drove a Panhard et Levassor cabriolet. At his property in Gisors outside Paris, Pauline enjoyed a rural and privileged childhood surrounded by her seven dogs and her favourite horse. She learned English, a rare accomplishment at the time, thanks to her Anglophile grandfather, who translated Shakespeare for pleasure, and who in fact died suddenly while working on *A Midsummer Night's Dream*.

Seeking to give her the best education possible, Pauline's father sent her to board at the Sainte-Clotilde convent school in Paris (today the Institut de La Tour), which was popular with bourgeois and aristocratic families, when she was eight years old. She disliked her blue uniform, and her school reports often contained remarks such as 'undisciplined' and 'badly behaved'. Later, at the convent Notre-Dame de Sion in Switzerland, where she was an unhappy boarder, she was to have her first experience as a milliner. One summer, the school hats were adorned with a monstrous white satin rosette. Without hesitation, Pauline coolly cut off her own and those of two friends. Summoned by the Mother Superior, she was ordered to say a dozen rosaries on her knees and to sew the rosettes back on.

The convent taught her to be quiet, to speak well, to obey and to do a three-step curtsy with eyes downcast. Since a natural ease of bearing was the recognized basis of a good upbringing ('In life, people will recognize you by these details,' she was forever being told), she was given lessons in deportment, learning how to walk elegantly on a slippery parquet floor, and in receiving friends for afternoon tea along with other similar exercises, all of which she found ridiculous.

Pauline Adam gives a lesson in elegance. Photograph by Lucien François at Studio Lavoisier.

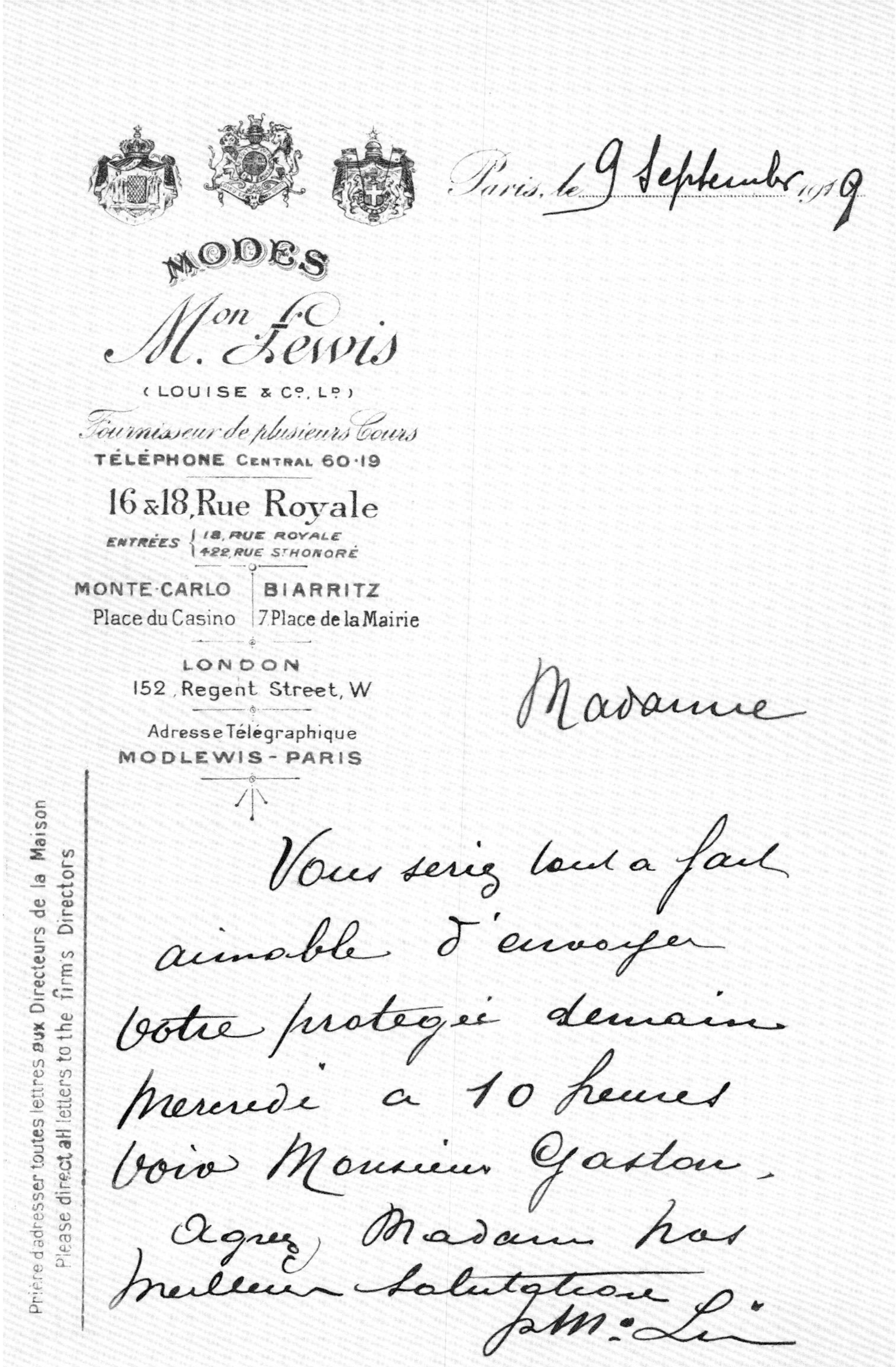

MODES

M^on L^C M. Lewis

(LOUISE & Co. L^D)

Fournisseur de plusieurs Cours

TÉLÉPHONE Central 60·19

16 & 18, Rue Royale

ENTRÉES | 18, RUE ROYALE
| 422, RUE ST HONORÉ

MONTE·CARLO | BIARRITZ
Place du Casino | 7 Place de la Mairie

LONDON
152, Regent Street, W

Adresse Télégraphique
MODLEWIS - PARIS

Prière d'adresser toutes lettres aux Directeurs de la Maison
Please direct all letters to the Firm's Directors

Paris, le 9 Septembre 1919

Madame

Vous serez tout a fait
aimable d'envoyer
votre protegée demain
mercredi a 10 heures
voir Monsieur Gaston.
Agreez Madame nos
meilleurs salutations
p.M. Le

Above: Pauline as a schoolgirl, 1916.

Opposite: Letter from Maison Lewis, September 1919.

In spite of her impatient and rebellious spirit, Pauline unconsciously acquired principles and a natural poise, which were to prove major assets in her future life. She even adopted the saying of one of her favourite teachers, Maggy de la Tour d'Auvergne: 'Never weary, never slack.'

Having passed her exams, she returned to her family in France. 'I lived in the countryside after I left the convent in Switzerland,' she recalled. 'I don't know how I had the strength to give up my pleasant idleness and consider going out to work…and in Paris! Did I want to surprise my family? To earn money to gain my independence? I think it was the lure of adventure that was my real motivation. Still, I knew I would have to sort out some difficulties at home. My father, whom I adored, had an absolute disdain for women who chose to work.'

Overcoming her reservations, Pauline was recommended by a family friend to the famous Maison Lewis, 'milliner to several courts', which had branches in Monte Carlo, Biarritz and London. Alongside Agnès and Caroline Reboux, Lewis dominated the creation of *haute mode* in Paris at the time (the term *haute mode* applied to the creation of hats by hand and to measure, in the same way that *haute couture* applied to clothes).

One morning in September 1919, Pauline was received by Monsieur Lewis in person in his salons on Rue Royale. The little schoolgirl in the ugly grey dress was to have her revenge. She had become a tall, slim young woman in a black velvet shift, with red lips and false eyelashes; at 1.74 metres (5 feet 8 inches) she was unusually tall for a woman at the time.

Monsieur Lewis and his chief assistant decided that Pauline had a 'head for hats' and hired her on the spot as an assistant house model. She immediately entered into the world of fashion, which was flourishing after the war years.

Raymond Marchand, Pauline's
future husband, 1914.

Pauline learned to slip into the
collection designs with the abstract
chic required by the style of this great
millinery house, which had several
hundred employees. Yet she quickly grew
impatient for a new adventure. Having
heard that a new millinery house, Brunet
et Verlaine, was moving to Rue de la
Paix and looking for a saleswoman, she
presented herself there and was hired by
a Monsieur Armand. She was twenty years
old. She tried her hand at designing hats,
learned to receive clients and even edited
a few press articles.

Two years later Pauline married her
first husband, Raymond Marchand. The
son of a lawyer, he was very handsome
with large, pale-blue eyes. He had studied
medicine for three years before becoming

caught up in the torment of the First
World War. Injured twice at Verdun,
he fought alongside British troops.
After the war, it was too late to continue
his medical studies and so Raymond
decided to become a print broker.
Gifted with a real talent for drawing and
caricature, he would produce accurate
and mischievous sketches of friends and
acquaintances.

Although by no means well off,
the young couple went out nearly every
evening, making friends with actors from
the Théâtre de l'Atelier in Montmartre,
where Charles Dullin put on both classic
and contemporary plays in a completely
innovative spirit. After the shows, the
performers would often spend pleasant
evenings dining at the home of the
Marchands.

Around the same time, Pauline was
also delighted to discover music hall
(Mistinguett and Maurice Chevalier
at the Casino de Paris, Josephine Baker at
the Folies Bergère), revues at the Palace
and jazz. These years immersed in Parisian
life were extremely happy and enriching,
and were doubtless responsible for
Pauline's special fondness for theatre and
stage costume throughout her career.

Pauline modelling for
Maison Lewis, 1919.

Starting Off

In 1925, in search of her own independence, Pauline Marchand decided to leave her comfortable position with Brunet et Verlaine and venture into hat design. Together with a wardrobe-mistress friend, she rented a tiny salon on Rue de la Pépinière. She was twenty-three when she proudly sold the first hat she had made with her own hands. She had talent and imagination; a small group of clients soon developed, enabling her to hire two employees.

In 1929, in response to her success, she moved her millinery house to an attractive apartment at 6 Rue de Ventadour, near the corner with Avenue de l'Opéra. It was at this time that she adopted the name 'Paulette' as a design label, finding it more modern than her elegant first name. Popularized by French and American film actresses, first names ending in 'ette' were in fashion (Ginette, Josette, Jeannette, Annette, Arlette, and so on). Later, she was to regret giving in to contemporary fashions, but she kept the pretty diminutive.

Paulette had given birth to a son in 1928. By now she was employing eight people in her atelier. A meeting with the ravishing Brazilian socialite Helena Ruy Barbosa – who invited her to come to the Ritz to present her designs – was to prove crucial.

Every spring, a stream of South Americans took up residence in Paris. The women – beautiful, charming and full of life – would run from one supplier to the next, seeking out the latest secret addresses of Paris fashion, before showing off their new clothes in the capitals and spa towns of Europe. Then, when winter returned to the northern hemisphere, they would head back to the sunshine of their homeland.

In the wake of Helena Ruy Barbosa, the whole Brazilian colony rushed to Paulette, soon followed by stylish women from other South American countries. 'From time to time, I would send parcels containing forty or more hats to each of them, in Brazil, Chile and Argentina,' she remembered. This was how she came to open a shop in Buenos Aires ten years later, which counted Eva Perón among its customers.

Asymmetric navy straw, 1937.

Paulette also developed a deep friendship with Maria de Sousa, later Maria Martins, the famous Brazilian writer and sculptor. Paulette kept up with Maria both in Paris and at her diplomat husband Carlos's successive postings abroad.

Brilliant years, successful years. Paulette gave birth to a second son in 1936, without slowing down her other activities – quite the contrary.

In this prewar period, women had never been so beautiful. Supremely elegant, they were mad about hats, which they ordered – sometimes by the dozen – for the events of their fashionable lifestyles. The Prix des Drags steeplechase at Auteuil, the Grand Prix de Paris at Longchamp, *concours d'élégance* motor shows, dinners at the Ritz, bridge at five o'clock, theatre visits, suppers at Bagatelle, costume balls… There were endless occasions for women in high society to flaunt their sophistication and originality.

Parisian *haute mode* was represented by numerous famous millinery houses, some long established, some new. Lucienne Rebaté had been running Reboux since the death of its founder in 1927; she was the undisputed specialist in structured shapes, like the Legroux Sœurs, who were very successful in the 1920s and were beginning to export their hats to the United States.

Suzy specialized in minuscule *bibis de singe*, tiny hats that were worn perched towards the front of the head. A pupil of Caroline Reboux, Rose Valois favoured clean lines, as did Jeanne Blanchot, who had trained as a sculptor, while Agnès took her inspiration from the work of modern painters. More technician than designer, Suzanne Talbot had a demure clientele, while the great Elsa Schiaparelli strove for sophisticated excess by mixing art and fashion: she liked to shock with her shoe hat, inkwell hat, cutlet hat and other surrealist inventions. Whether or not her designs were flattering was of little importance to her.

Other significant names included Maria Guy, Blanche et Simone, Rose Descat, the creative Albouy and Claude Saint-Cyr, who, after starting out as a seamstress in various Paris workrooms, launched her own label in 1937 and later became the official milliner to Queen Elizabeth II under the aegis of the couturier Norman Hartnell.

Faced with these diverse competitors, each with their own image and identity, Paulette developed her characteristic style of refinement and casual charm. She created *bibis-jardins*, perched high and tilted forwards; soft pillboxes and boaters decorated with posies; asymmetric capelines in fine straw; and all sorts of felt skullcaps enhanced with pin tucks and gathers, tilted graciously forwards or to the side, little miracles of balance and lightness. For evening wear, she attached aigrettes and feathers onto velvet *calots* (small brimless hats). She was fond of veils, which had become one of her trademarks, as they 'brightened the eyes and added a sense of mystery'. Her veils covered the face or hung from the back of the hat in folds.

In addition to her talent as a designer, Paulette had acquired an unfailing technique. Yet her atelier, which now comprised twelve seamstresses, was no longer able to fulfil the growing number of orders. As 'the' milliner of the moment, she needed to add a new dimension to her millinery house.

The adventure was risky, although a fortune-teller – a pseudo Hindu princess – had predicted she would be successful. 'I was taught,' Paulette was to recount, remembering her time as a horsewoman, 'to steer my horse towards the fence. I had the choice between risking breaking my neck and doing nothing.' She therefore invested all her savings in a new project.

Paulette with her eldest son, Jean-Pierre, 1932.

Opposite, clockwise
from top left: Straw boater
topped with a cloud of
tulle, fruit and an ear
of wheat, 1937.

Small hat with posy,
1938. Illustration by
Jacques Demachy.

Small purple veiled
straw decorated with a
cellophane bird, 1938.

Below: Flat, black straw
with two-coloured plume,
1937.

3

The 1940s

In February 1939, six months before the declaration of war, Paulette moved her salons and workrooms to 63 Avenue Victor-Emmanuel III (later renamed Avenue Franklin D. Roosevelt). Jean-Claude Dondel, the architect behind the Palais de Tokyo (a museum of modern and contemporary art in Paris), was commissioned to fit out the two vast floors. The spacious salons opened on to each other, and a carpet with large black-and-white checks was used to harmonize the space, which was punctuated with white plaster columns, gilt frames and black leather chairs, and illuminated by a monumental crystal chandelier.

The fashion illustrator and designer Christian Bérard, with whom Paulette had become friends, designed the eye-catching logo of ostrich feathers and wheat ears that was to feature on her hat boxes and publicity for 'Paulette Modes'.

Her friends Carlos and Maria Martins had left the Brazilian Embassy in Brussels for that in Washington. Sensing the scale

One of the salons of Paulette Modes, decorated by Jean-Claude Dondel, 1939.

of the conflict that was about to begin, they begged Paulette to join them in the United States with her family. Of course, she refused. France was sitting on a time bomb, but this did not stop the stream of parties and balls. The magazines heralded spring and summer fashions that were as feminine and joyous as ever. Women clung on to frivolity as to a life raft. In her biography of Françoise Sagan, Marie-Dominique Lelièvre evokes the imprudence of the writer's mother: 'On the evening of the declaration of war, Marie Quoirez left her family in Cajarc to fetch her collection of hats made by the milliner Paulette from Paris.'

But a few weeks later, there was an exodus. Paulette, who took refuge in south-west France with her children, was concerned about her staff. *Vogue* chose the title 'Adieu la mode' for its December 1939 editorial, which recalled that the clothing industry employed one million people and the couture industry twenty-five thousand, plus spinners, weavers, narrow-weavers, braiders and embroiderers. For his part, Prime Minister Paul Reynaud declared that France should continue to export, and that couturiers

Clockwise from top left: Veiled silk bonnet
embellished with silk flowers, 1945.

Hats by Paulette, dresses by Bruyère and Robert
Piguet, 1943. Illustration by André Delfau.

'Afternoon tea chez Carrère', 1943.

'At the Louvre', hats by Paulette, 1944.
Illustration by André Delfau.

Opposite: A Paulette advertisement for
fashion magazines, 1941.

had a social duty to provide a living for their employees.

Paulette chose to return to Paris at the end of 1940. The capital was occupied. The German authorities planned to transfer the Paris fashion industry to Berlin or Vienna, but the couturier Lucien Lelong, president of the Chambre Syndicale de la Haute Couture, managed to retain ninety-two houses in Paris (this number was later reduced to fifty-four), thereby avoiding unemployment for the thousands of employees and artisans who worked for them. A skilful negotiator, he persuaded the occupiers that the

couturiers and seamstresses would lose all their talent if they were to leave Paris.

Lelong secured special rules for haute couture, and customers were given cards disguised as ration tickets that allowed them to buy from prestigious fashion houses. Nevertheless, there were restrictions on fabric, as three-quarters of production was requisitioned by Germany. Yardage for coats and tailored dresses was also strictly regulated, as was the composition of collections (with the maximum of a hundred designs per collection falling to just sixty towards the end of the war).

Left: Turquoise silk-jersey turban, 1943.

Right: Green draped woollen printed
with red leaves, 1941.

It was under these conditions that Paulette reopened her workrooms and tracked down her seamstresses and saleswomen. Strangely, the theatres, restaurants, cabarets and cinemas were all full. The races at Auteuil and Longchamp resumed at the end of 1940. Charity galas, teas at Carrère and dinners at Maxim's continued unabated. Bit by bit, members of high society regained something of their former fashionable lifestyles, providing business to couturiers and milliners.

Once again, fashion stayed abreast of innovation. Paulette despaired of 'those ridiculous little discs held on by a piece of elastic, which look more like petticoat accessories than hats' (the aforementioned *bibis de singe*). They were still popular, but seemed completely anachronistic. Paulette decided to innovate and came up with new shapes, extending hats with scarves made of tulle, organza and wool, depending on the season. 'Paulette makes hats that begin on the head but end in mystery. They release long, wide folds that curl around the shoulders, resembling a light cape, or they have turned-up brims and loops. It is an adorable fashion,' wrote Lucien François in *L'Art et la Mode* in 1941.

One evening, finding herself unprepared as she was about to set off for a restaurant, Paulette improvised a turban by wrapping a black jersey scarf around her head and fixing it in place with six gold pins.

The compliments she received and the popularity of the turban with fellow diners led her to suspect that women could find this kind of headgear appealing. It was very practical when riding a bicycle – the only means of transport possible at the time – and soft enough to be slipped into a pocket.

The small collection of turbans that she developed in her workrooms required days of research and refinement to ensure the hats did not resemble Hindu headdresses. The line was very modern as the high drape pulled the turban back off the face and the back section was extremely high.

Two pretty clients, Annette Fabry and the young Duchess of Elchingen, dared to sport these designs at Maxim's.

The '*turban-bicyclette*' ('bicycle turban'), as it was called by Paulette, was launched. It became an institution, star of the *journées de l'élégance à bicyclette*, the bicycle-wear fashion shows that took place in the Bois de Boulogne in place of the *concours d'élégance* motor shows, which were impossible because of the lack of petrol.

Later, Paulette was to recall dinners at which 'elegant women would arrive, having struggled through the wind and

Silk turban in shocking pink, 1944.

Clockwise, from top left:
Checked surah turban with
a base of plaited straw, 1943.

Striped surah turban topped
with a straw blackbird, 1944.

Draped turban finished
with foxtail, 1942. Illustration
by Roger Rouffiange.

Above: Voluminous turban mounted with a
nest of roses encased in a fine veil, 1942.

Opposite: Dark blue jersey turban, 1942.

rain to get there. A quick glance in the mirror on entering, a comb of the hair, a dab of powder…and then they would slip on a fabulous turban, produced from the bicycle's pannier, and make a triumphant entrance.'

Small local milliners followed suit with all the more enthusiasm as the turban was such an effective solution to the problems of hairstyling in the current times of shortage. 'Not only had having one's hair set become a whole to-do, but turbans were fashionable. They took the place of both hat and hairstyle,' wrote one of their most famous devotees, Simone de Beauvoir, in her autobiography *The Prime of Life*. Compared with the extravagances to come, these innovative designs were to remain among Paulette's most demure.

Although the German occupiers had imposed strict quotas on yardage of fabric, hats had the advantage in that they could be made from unusable offcuts, unusual materials and all kinds of other components found in old stock. The resulting edifices of flowers and stuffed birds horrified Christian Dior, who during the war was working as a designer for Lucien Lelong. In his memoirs,

Navy-blue felt Phrygian cap wrapped in ivory crêpe, 1942.

he deplored the fashion for 'enormous pouffes that defy common sense'.

Paulette admitted to getting carried away herself by the rampant escalating extravagance: 'My imagination was my worst enemy. My designs were sometimes too excessive to be tasteful. I learned to stop before I had lost the sense of balance.'

Nests and structures of flowers, feathers and ribbons that made the wearer look like a walking hat, coupled with clothes with excessive shoulders, allowed women to forget the shortage of materials and the limitations of their wardrobes, to vary their outfits and thus overcome the gloom of the war years. This eccentricity was, nonetheless, perceived as a provocation by the occupying authorities. Paulette and a few fellow milliners were summoned to the *Kommandantur* (German command post) and told in no uncertain terms to moderate their designs or their houses would be closed. The order fell on deaf ears and the hats remained agents of disorder until the end.

Like the German occupiers, the Vichy government was also indignant about the vanity and frivolity of French women, who were at pains to be elegant in spite of the circumstances. They followed to the letter the recommendations of the fashion magazines, which, with the exception of *Vogue* and *Femina*, were still being published. *Femme Chic, L'Officiel de la Couture, L'Art et la Mode, Silhouette* and the very chic *Album du Figaro* all highlighted the designs of the couturiers in particular, since despite regular threats of closure, the couture houses were extremely busy. Their regular clients had returned, boosted by the wives of dignitaries and businessmen who had grown rich under the occupation.

True, Chanel closed her house, and Mainbocher returned to New York and Edward Molyneux to London. Christian Dior and Pierre Balmain, both trained by Robert Piguet, were at the time designers with Lucien Lelong, whose fluid drapes and folds were very popular. Madame Grès modelled her magic folds of fine jersey on Greek sculpture; Cristóbal Balenciaga was already known for the

precision of his cuts (in 1944, the houses of Grès and Balenciaga were ordered to close as they had exceeded their fabric allocation. The intervention of the Spanish Embassy allowed Balenciaga to resume his activity). Jeanne Lanvin stayed faithful to her refined style; the ambitious Jacques Fath began his brilliant career; and Maggy Rouff, Madeleine de Rauch and Marcel Rochas tried their hands at 'sporty' lines, practical for cycling and more suitable for a world undergoing change. Rochas was responsible for the silhouette that predominated throughout the war: broad shoulders, narrow waists, short skirts that barely covered the knees, with gathers and drapes on skirts and bodices, and bouffant sleeves. Three-quarter-length coats and fur-lined jackets emphasized the shape.

Elise Daniels, turban by Paulette, Paris, 1948. Photograph by Richard Avedon.

Following her return to Paris, Paulette was introduced to the couturier Robert Piguet, who asked her to create hats to accompany his designs. She was to participate in the fevered preparation of the Piguet collections, bringing her imagination to bear on the sharp cuts of the suits and the fluidity of the dresses (including his trademark navy-crêpe designs) until the closure of the Maison Piguet in 1951.

This man of the world, a sophisticated designer with whom she developed a deep friendship, introduced her to his circle of friends, to whom she also became close. The actresses Gabrielle Dorziat and Madeleine Renaud, the actor and director Jean-Louis Barrault, the poet Jean Cocteau, the shoe designer Roger Vivier, the painter Edouard MacAvoy and, above all, the divine Christian Bérard, painter, fashion illustrator and theatre designer, who in turn was to present her to Cecil Beaton, which was to prove yet another significant introduction.

Above: Robert Piguet by Leonor Fini, oil on canvas, 1950.

Opposite: Robert Piguet and Paulette at a fitting, 1950. Photograph by Willy Rizzo.

Chapeau de Paulette, jersey Vali-
sère, exclusivité Sainclair. La fan-
taisie de tout le personnage est
parfois dans le seul chapeau.
Maître d'une architecture, il s'en-
hardit jusqu'à ces couleurs d'éten-
dard. Triomphant, imprévu et
comme frissonné à l'instant dans
le jersey, le drap, la toile à fleurs
par une main habile, à moins que
ce ne soit le vent. De jour, de nuit,
des oiseaux volent derrière lui.
L'un s'y pose, attend les autres et
leur fait signe de sa plume. Mais
c'est déjà le temps des papillons,
sortant de leurs chrysalides de
tulle.

Postwar Celebrity

4

ollowing the Liberation in August 1944, the blue, white and red of the French flag was everywhere: in fashion, shops and advertisements, and out on the streets. Paulette created a range of large tricolour berets, symbolizing the return of national pride. She did not abandon the famous turban that had established her name, but she was keen to make technical adjustments and update the style.

Struck by the elegance of the turbans worn by the Moroccan soldiers she saw marching down the Champs-Elysées, Paulette went to their camp and asked the colonel in charge of the Tabors to show her how to roll up the fabric so she could understand the dynamic of the drape. Over time, however, her reputation as the 'queen of the turban' came to exasperate her. Eventually she was to include just one turban design in each of her collections; it always bore the name 'Ali' and was dated with the relevant year.

At the beginning of 1945, Paulette was an enthusiastic participant in an touring exhibition project devised by the Chambre Syndicale de la Haute Couture, which aimed to relaunch French fashion

Above: Oriental turban in turquoise silk jersey, 1946.

Opposite: Large tricolour beret made in celebration of the Liberation, 1946. Illustration by Pierre-Laurent Brenot from a contemporary publication.

'Palais Royal', from the exhibition 'Théâtre de la Mode'
at the Musée des Arts Décoratifs, Paris, 1945.
Set design by André Dignimont.

'La Rue de la Paix', from the exhibition
'Théâtre de la Mode' at the Musée des Arts
Décoratifs, Paris, 1945. Set design by
Louis Touchagues.

abroad. Proceeds from the sale of tickets and programmes were to be paid to the Moroccan relief organization L'Entraide Nationale.

The couturier Robert Ricci, an influential member of the Chambre Syndicale, had the idea to present the Winter 1945/46 collections on miniature mannequins, in the style of the fashion dolls used in the eighteenth century to present Parisian outfits to foreign courts each season. In collaboration with the artist Jean Saint-Martin, the illustrator Eliane Bonabel invented supple wire figures that could be bent into all kinds of poses. The small, white plaster heads of the 237 figurines were made by the Catalan sculptor Joan Rebull Torroja.

Christian Bérard was in charge of scenography and artistic direction, and came up with the idea of placing the mannequins in thirteen miniature theatre sets, with backdrops painted by famous artists including Jean Cocteau, Louis Touchagues, Jean-Denis Malclès, André Dignimont and Georges Wakhévitch.

Forty couturiers, thirty-six milliners, plus hairdressers, bootmakers, glovemakers and jewellers, succeeded in dressing the 70 cm (28 in.) tall mannequins with the utmost precision. Paulette produced minuscule feathers and flowers for the hats she had made to match some of the suits, coats and evening dresses. Lighting by the ballet director and scenarist Boris Kochno added a touch of magic to the sets, which depicted different parts of Paris and in which the characters seemed to move against the background of music specially composed by Henri Sauguet.

The exhibition, which took place in March 1945 in the Musée des Arts Décoratifs in the Louvre's Pavillon de Marsan, was a huge success: 100,000 visitors attended, raising 1,000,000 francs for L'Entraide Nationale.

After the long years of deprivation, French elegance also fascinated abroad. The exhibition travelled to Barcelona, Stockholm and Copenhagen before arriving in London, where 120,000 visitors came to admire the 'Fantasy of Fashion' (the English name for the 'Théâtre de la Mode').

In spring 1946, the American leg of the tour (New York, Boston, San Francisco) was based around the presentation of the summer haute couture collection. Once again, Parisian couturiers, milliners and artisans went to extreme lengths to dress their wire figurines. Other artists and designers (including Emilio Terry) created new sets. Here, too, the reception was triumphant, as it would prove to be in Montreal, Buenos Aires, Vienna and, finally, Leeds.

Above: The actress Anouk Aimée
wearing a cap encrusted with fantasy
jewels, 1948. Photograph by Willy
Maywald.

Opposite: Evening headdress, 1946.
Photograph by Willy Maywald.

PAULETTE

Clockwise from top:
Large straw tied with
a patterned lawn
handkerchief, 1947.

Bonnet with large printed
brim and flecked veil, 1945.
Illustration by Pierre Louchel.

Foulard and jersey turban,
1940. Illustration by
Christian Bérard.

This original promotional campaign played a decisive role in the recovery of French couture in the immediate postwar period, notably following the sensational presentation of the exhibition at the Metropolitan Museum in New York.

After a five-year break, the publication of *Vogue* resumed. Professional buyers and their agents returned. Paulette Modes now employed 120 people in its three workrooms and salons, including seven saleswomen and three permanent house models: Renée de Béarn, Maureen O'Connor and Suzanne de Douville-Maillefeu. Paulette – 'my modest *modiste*' as Robert Piguet affectionately referred to her – was creating straw hats with wide, turned-up brims, elaborate berets, 'halo-effect' hats worn on the back of the head, capelines kept in place by fine veils tied under the chin, and *calottes évidées* (wide-brimmed hats with open crowns). In 1946, she invented her famous 'pillbox', a small, round, brimless hat with a low, flat crown that Jackie Kennedy was to popularize twenty years later by wearing it on the back of her head.

Paulette's hundred or so seamstresses made up to eight hundred hats a month, exclusively by hand, for Paris's fashionable elite and its beautiful visitors. 'Following the Liberation, Americans rushed to Paris to buy hats,' she recalled. 'It was crazy.

As well as the couturiers who had their own specialized hat ateliers, there were also a good ten houses of *haute mode* in business. I had the largest clientele by far.'

Unlike other milliners, who employed illustrators, Paulette never worked from sketches: she designed her shapes directly on a wooden hat block that was covered with canvas so materials could be pinned to it easily. Inspiration could be immediate or could take days to crystallize.

One of her workrooms would then receive a sparterie version of the design – a rigid shape that was used as a mould for the hat. Fabric made of plant fibre (sparterie) and lined with stiff cotton muslin was moistened and worked using a heated 'egg iron' (a cast-iron egg with a pointed end). Pieces of sparterie were sewn on to reinforce the double folds and a piece of brass wire was used to consolidate the edges of the shape, which was then stiffened using heated gutta–percha paste. (This time-consuming method of production is no longer in use today as milliners have abandoned sparterie in favour of working from untreated canvas.) The extremely hard mould was then used to make a maximum of ten hats in different materials and infinite variations.

Once the sparterie versions had been pinned to wooden 'dolls', felt was stretched manually, using first steam from a kettle, then a damp cloth. Velvet was worked on the bias using egg irons. Skeins of Italian straw braid were sewn by hand, in spirals and with small hidden stitches, hugging the shape of the sparterie. It took six or seven hours of fine sewing to finish a hat.

Moulds made of limewood had no place in *haute mode* according to Paulette, except for a few basic forms that were used to make the sparterie moulds. She thought they should be reserved for mass production and was wary of them, believing that they encouraged plagiarism (block-makers had no qualms about showing the moulds to rival houses).

However, Paulette did use limewood moulds to carry out large orders for professional buyers such as the famous milliner Otto Lucas of London and then, after Lucas's tragic death in an aeroplane accident, the House of Dolorès. Although the buyers had exclusive rights to the design, Paulette was so afraid of plagiarism that she did not allow them to attend the presentations of her new collections unless they agreed to buy a minimum of three sparterie moulds, one hat and a specific number of labels.

In order to meet these large-scale orders, 'Madame Paulette' – as she was now referred to in the profession –

enlisted the services of Italo and Lorenzo Ré, Italian block-makers with a gift for sculpting and a sense of proportion that she particularly appreciated. (Lorenzo Ré is one of only two block-makers still practising in Europe. Using only a gouge, file and sandpaper, he sculpts silky, light-coloured hat blocks that are surprisingly sensual. Not surprisingly, he works for some of the leading French and British milliners.)

When Paulette wanted a mould, she would go to the workroom on Place des Victoires and the block-maker would shape the mould in limewood according to her sparterie design, rather than basing it on a simple sketch, as was generally the case. She forbade anyone else to enter the workroom while she was there, staying with the craftsman for two to three hours while the rough shape was sculpted. Even today, Renzo Ré still marvels at the perfection of the sparterie moulds she used to bring to him: 'true sculptures', he says. She was, and still is in his eyes, 'the greatest'.

Close-fitting sculpted cap in brown felt with a grosgrain ribbon bow fastened with a clip, 1947.

Green leaves and camellias adorn
white gloves. Roger Model.

Loops of pink and white
straw fixed by a glittering
jewel. Paulette.

A sheer-brimmed beauty in black
organdie gently shades the face. Paulette.

Above: Rose quartz hat in
amethyst panne velvet lined
with black with a fur stole by
Molyneux, 1950. Photograph by
Henry Clarke.

Opposite: Sheer-brimmed hat in
black organdie by Paulette, with
gloves by Roger Model, 1952.
Illustration by Jacques Demachy.

5

Famous Fittings

Paulette's three workrooms were spread over the two floors of 63 Avenue Franklin D. Roosevelt, alongside the storeroom, where fabrics, flowers, feathers and veils were kept in boxes.

The overcrowded workrooms were subject to a strict hierarchy. In each room, one of Paulette's three chief assistants (first Monette, Suzy and Madeleine, then later Mimi, Jeannette and Léone) oversaw a long table. Next to them they each had two second assistants, six highly qualified finishers, six finishers with a medium amount of experience (six years in general), ten finishers with less experience (three to four years), and four young apprentices at the end of the table. These last would pick up pins, heat the egg irons with gas and fetch rolls of fabric from the storeroom. Workspaces were in order of seniority, in accordance with this hierarchy. The milliners worked on their knees and on the wooden dolls. In theory, the qualified finishers made the hats from start to finish, while the second assistants

Paulette in one of her workrooms, 1952.

attached veils and trimmings. The chief assistants supervised and knew exactly how to correct any imperfections after fittings.

Each of the three workrooms had its own speciality: the workroom run by Madame Monette, who was an expert with the egg iron, did not handle felts; Madame Suzy's workroom worked with freer forms; while Madame Madeleine's workroom was more traditional. The star workroom was undoubtedly that run by Monette, who was an exceptional technician. Paulette sat beside her to work when she was not required in the other workrooms or in the salons, where she advised clients on hat choices and supervised measuring (every client had her own measurement card) and fittings.

Established customers tried on their new hats in two stages: first the crown and then the brim, fixed on the grosgrain headband. The hat was literally made on the client's head: it was a unique, bespoke item. Paulette, the saleswoman, the chief assistant and often the second assistant would all take part in the fitting.

At the second fitting, the shape was expected to be perfect, as pure as a sculpture and very light. It was at this point that Paulette decided on the trimmings, which were an integral part of the design.

The choice was between ribbons, flowers, leaves and feathers of all sorts. Trimmings were made by master craftsmen and women at firms such as Fromentin, Legeron and Lemarié, which are still in business today. André Lemarié, who inherited a house that was founded in 1880, started out as a *plumassier*, working with ornamental feathers, but soon branched out into making decorative flowers before taking over the atelier of Juliette Barbier, a specialist in the reproduction of natural flowers in silk.

Lemarié used to take his latest creations to Paulette's salons to show them to her; she loved to go through the designs intended for haute couture, and was enthusiastic about his extravagant use of aigrettes made of cockerel feathers, goose quills and scores of other feathers from domestic birds, the use of which was in line with the requirements of the Washington Convention on endangered species, which was strictly adhered to in the United States.

Success did not alter Paulette's routine. She continued to make hats herself, which she loved to do, sitting down regularly at one of the large workroom tables,

always elegant in her triple row of pearls. A technical expert at every stage in the production process, she would modify a design along the way, adding in details and embroidering like an artisan.

Nevertheless, her presence was always required by clients wanting her opinion, some advice or a personal touch, and especially by those who were famous or of high social standing. One day, a petite American, blond and pretty, was waiting in front of a mirror. She looked shy and lost, and Paulette went up to her and asked if she could help. The young woman ordered several hats and briefly gave her name: Mrs 'Fortoo'. In the afternoon, the American Embassy called and asked to speak to the saleswoman who had helped Mrs Henry Ford II. Nobody knew who had served this important client, until Paulette realized that she had. They both laughed at this mistake for a long time to come.

Paulette selects a photograph from a contact sheet, 1948.

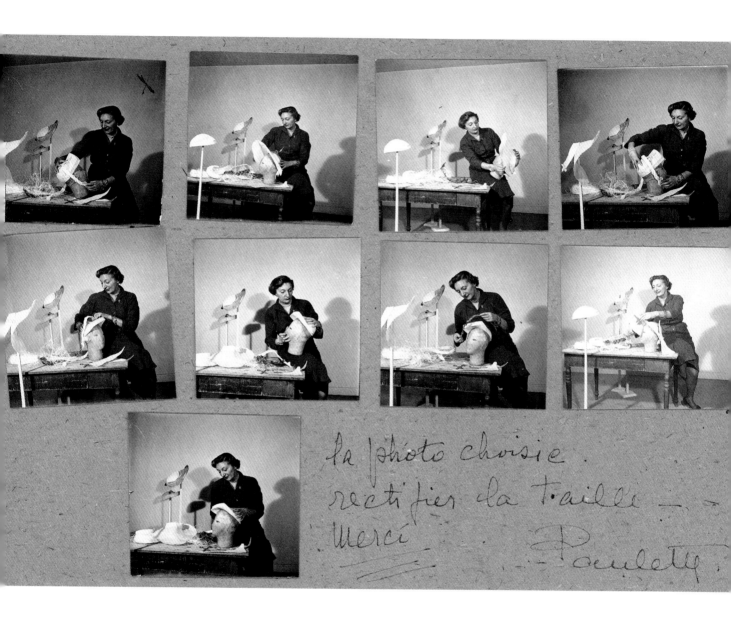

la photo choisie.
rectifier la taille —
merci
Paulette

Above and opposite: Small straw veiled toques topped with rose bouquets, 1948.

In the noisy and crowded salons, fitters and saleswomen, often irritated and overwhelmed, would run around like mice in a cage. The arrival of Madame Paulette, as they too called her, would put an immediate stop to the turmoil and the impatient squeaking of the clients.

Some customers were faithful for seasons, years, even their whole lives. They would buy hats for a particular event or one for all occasions. This was an era when women changed hats several times a day and considered them an essential fashion accessory. 'It's crazy what some women expect from a hat!' Paulette would sigh, amused by their expressions and gestures in front of the fitting-room mirror.

There was no question that a hat full of mischief or spirit offered the wearer the opportunity to try out a different personality, but they had to be up to the challenge. Hats were 'a way of behaving', and Paulette advised shy women against wearing them.

A superb judge of her clients' characters, Paulette identified their type straight away: the invisible women who lived in the shadow of a great man; the strong women who wanted to be weak; the short women who wanted to be tall and the tall women who would bend over in a bid to shrink; the women with fat

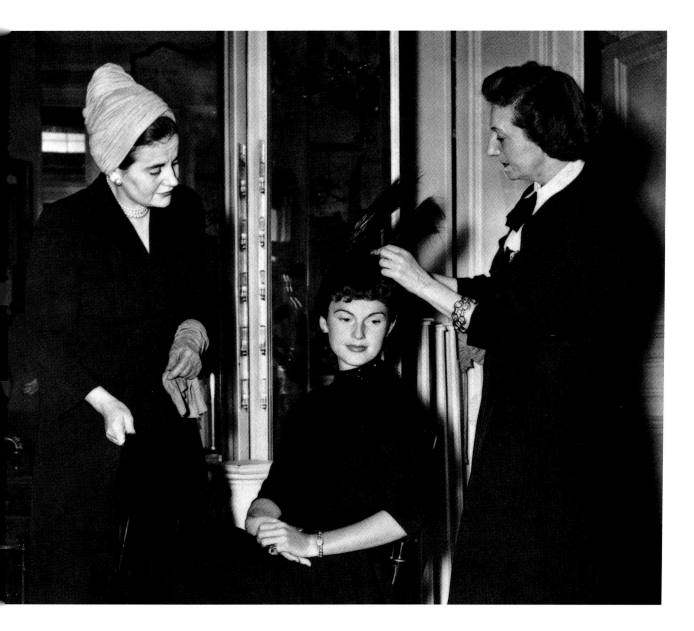

Fitting for the 'Rabbit Ears' hat,
immortalized by Richard Avedon,
1949 (see page 15).

cheeks who sucked them in and wished they looked like Marlene Dietrich; the ageing women who wanted to stay young; the impossible women who strained the nerves and made the saleswomen cry… More generally, Paulette believed that all her female clients fell into one of four categories. There were the saintly, who had a modest demeanour in spite of their responsibilities, such as the owner of a tool factory who had been caring for her sick husband for ten years and never showed a hint of impatience. The smitten, on the other hand, were in a state of permanent anguish and returned their hats at the smallest criticism from their husband or lover (who sometimes accompanied them to the salon, declaring remorsefully: 'I love the hats you make for my wife!'). The domineering, who wasted no time thumping 'I love it' or 'I hate it', were less entertaining; unlike, finally, the crazy, for whom Paulette had a particular weakness, such as the beauty who thought nothing of undergoing surgery to her ears so she could carry off a large straw pancake hat that had caught her fancy.

Not forgetting the miserly clients, such as the fabulously wealthy bourgeois woman who asked Paulette to make her an evening toque for the following day. In the space of a few minutes, the milliner rustled up a miracle of grace

Blond straw with velvet anemones and gouza feathers, 1946.

and elegance. The client was delighted, but the saleswoman came over to Paulette and whispered: 'Madame thinks it's terribly expensive for a piece of veil, a flower and some ribbons.' 'That's not a problem,' Paulette retorted, calmly undoing her creation. She held out the rose, ribbons and veil to the mortified client: 'This will only cost you one franc!'

Paulette retained this gaiety and irony for a long time; she knew when to be tough and when to conceal her influence. The magazine *Collections* painted the picture of a 'tall brunette with a low voice, a mixture of charm and authority, a surprising presence, unaffectedness combined with natural elegance'. She was nearly eighty when Eve Ruggieri wrote in *Elle*: 'Her eyes reflect a hint of independence, of mischief, of leisurely nonchalance, all seasoned with a pinch of provocation.' Always dressed simply, in brown or black in the winter (with her famous rows of pearls) and beige in the summer, she sometimes accessorized with precious gems or baroque jewelry. All the same, some of her sober suits were signed 'Balenciaga'.

Paulette, April 1948.

Above: Flat capeline, 1951. Photograph by Bill Brandt.

Opposite: Mrs George Mardikian in the 'Mme Curie',
a simple fabric bowler in Dumbo grey, tied under the chin
and veiled in matching grey, with a velveteen coat and
gloves by Robert Piguet, 1949.

America Comes Calling

At the end of the war, Paulette became friends with Marie-Louise Bousquet, a great friend of Christian Bérard and head of the Paris office of *Harper's Bazaar*. An intellectual and socialite, and a vivacious character, she received writers, artists, society people and diplomats every Thursday. Her salon at 3 Place du Palais-Bourbon ('where up the flights of stairs have winded many a celebrity', according to the writer Philippe Jullian) was known as the antechamber of the Académie Française and the Ministry of Foreign Affairs. Her fashion curiosity and sense of style meant that she called the shots with the couturiers.

In spring 1946, the legendary editor-in-chief of *Harper's Bazaar* Carmel Snow arrived in Paris; she was the first person to sense that the city's years of isolation had not affected the vitality of French design. Her sharp eyes took in the work of every couture house; she knew how to spot talent and how to encourage it.

Paulette on board the *George Washington* during its Atlantic crossing, 1946.

When Paulette was introduced to Carmel Snow by Marie-Louise Bousquet, the American agreed immediately to attend the presentation of her new collection. 'After the show had finished,' Paulette wrote in her private notes, 'Carmel Snow asked to see me. I was very intimidated, like a novice. I felt her blue eyes resting on me, vague and precise at the same time. She took my arm gently: "You must come to New York, Paulette. I promise I will help you. But…don't lose time." Marie-Louise, who was present at our meeting, looked at me with her irresistible expression, the silent laugh that twists her mouth slightly. I embraced her with affection and gratitude.'

The opportunity for adventure was too tempting: Paulette packed her bags, like the many couturiers and businessmen who were also fascinated by America. Unable to secure a seat on an aeroplane, she settled for the *George Washington*, a Liberty ship, where she was one of a few civilians rubbing shoulders with the American soldiers on board. After a ten-day crossing, which was both gruelling and exhilarating, the ship reached New York in an atmosphere of celebration.

'We were escorted by two small boats full of richly attired musicians, who were blowing into their brass instruments for all they were worth,' Paulette recalled. 'In the fog, the city was as silent as an enormous cathedral with multiple spires. I was choked with emotion.'

Carlos and Maria Martins came to meet her on the quay, waiting in the middle of the crowd that swarmed around the ship. She followed them to Washington, where they threw a huge cocktail party in her honour at the Brazilian Embassy. When the journalists present expressed surprise that the Parisian milliner was not wearing a hat, just topaz hairclips, Paulette replied that pastry cooks did not eat cakes every day and jewellers' wives avoided showy jewelry – an answer that was to establish her image in the local press.

An established sculptor, Maria Martins invited an unusual yet attractive mix of guests to her receptions, including millionaires, politicians and foreign artists who had settled in America. This was how Paulette came to meet Fernand Léger, Marcel Duchamp and Alexander Calder, who were all to have a profound effect on her.

Back in New York, she discovered a vibrant arts scene and lots of her old American friends. Carmel Snow kept her promise and took her under her wing. There were lunches at the Colony and dinners at Le Pavillon and other restaurants frequented by café society. Paulette was able to observe American fashion at her leisure; women were still wearing the tiny flowery *bibis* from before the war. 'America was rich; poor, we were luxurious,' she once said. Paulette thus began to suspect the potential of opening up an establishment in the United States, and she laid down her first markers.

Velvet skullcap with diamante clip, 1950.
Photograph by Horst P. Horst.

High Society

After a stay of one month that proved highly encouraging, Paulette returned from the United States to her Parisian workrooms in good spirits. Paulette Modes had held up well in her absence and was still as popular as ever with clients. But it was time for a complete rethink: fashions were changing and becoming both more demure and more eccentrically elegant.

In 1947, Christian Dior, who had set up his couture house a year earlier with the support of the industrialist Marcel Boussac, started a revolution. After the short skirts and broad shoulders of the war years, he invented a new silhouette of extreme femininity: an ultra-narrow waist, soft shoulders and very long, full skirts requiring phenomenal quantities of fabric – up to 18 metres (59 feet) of material. Carmel Snow dubbed this alluring shape, which called either for small refined hats, or for large capelines with flat crowns and Asian-inspired triangle hats without frills and flounces, the 'New Look'. It was

a magnificent period for Parisian high fashion; milliners had at their disposal felt, silk velvet, fine Italian straw, gleaming paillasson, baku (a very delicate straw), and feathers of all sorts: heron, pheasant, cockerel, ostrich, egret and bird of paradise.

At the time, no woman could go out without a hat or *en cheveux* ('wearing her hair'), as it was called. Hats were worn at the races, at cocktail parties and soirées, and in particular at restaurants, where they were especially important. As Paulette was constantly repeating: 'At the dining table, the women are all hats and jewelry!'

1948 saw the launch of the first '*Grande Saison de Paris*': Wednesdays at Les Ambassadeurs, Fridays at Maxim's, plus theatre evenings, fashionable soirées and charity galas: the '*Bal du Panache*' given by Lady Diana Cooper at the British Embassy, the '*Bal des Petits Lits Blancs*' at the Opéra, the '*Bal des Oiseaux*' at the Palais Rose, the '*Bal d'Hiver*' at the Palais de Glace, balls at the Hotel Lambert in aid of the Polish community in Paris, and so on.

The aristocracy, together with fashionable society and dilettantes, revived themed costume balls, which

Asymmetric straw with a sweeping brim, 1949. Photograph by Arik Nepo.

Top: Fitted bird-wings headdress in mahogany felt, 1949.

Above: Large straw with turned-up brim, 1947.

Top: Lightweight hat worn to one side and adorned with a cloud of tulle.

Above: Large, black velvet bonnet embellished with multicoloured bird-of-paradise feathers, 1946. Illustration by Jacques Demachy.

Top: Black velvet wings covered with bird-of-paradise feathers, 1947.

Above: Black velvet capeline crowned with bird-of-paradise feathers, 1947. Illustration by Pierre Mourgue.

Opposite: 'Chez Maxim's', 1946. Illustration by René Gruau.

had been extremely popular between the wars. Popular artists and writers, and distinguished foreigners were invited to these private parties, where meticulous care was paid to the costumes, masks and hairstyles, and to the guests' entrances, which featured two or more people in the form of a tableau vivant.

Count Etienne de Beaumont held several of these costume balls in his beautiful private town house on Rue Masseran, spending all his time preparing these frivolous, joyful occasions. Equally entertaining were the masquerades given by Baron and Baroness de Cabrol, as were the balls given by the Noailles in their sumptuous residence on Place des Etats-Unis.

In their wake, the formidable 'Hollywood gossip' Elsa Maxwell organized soirées in New York, Paris and Biarritz that were attended by swarms of cinema stars, millionaires, politicians, socialites and artists of all kinds, a café society that the Duchess of Westminster dubbed 'Nescafé Society'.

But the 'party of the century' was undeniably the ball thrown by the flamboyant, multi-millionaire art collector Carlos de Beistegui at Palazzo Labia in Venice in September 1951. The costumes worn by the four hundred guests, who came from all over Europe, were inspired by paintings and wall hangings from the eighteenth century: the revellers looked as if they had stepped out of the Tiepolo frescoes decorating the palace walls.

In the middle of the night, the guests, dressed in their splendid costumes, went out and mingled with the ordinary Venetians who had gathered in the piazza outside the palace. The ball continued like this in an atmosphere of dizzying gaiety until daybreak.

Keen to compete with Beistegui's splendour, the Marquis de Cuevas organized a grandiose costume ball at the Chiberta golf club outside Biarritz two years later. The enchanting vision of the Marquis's ballet company dancing *Swan Lake* on a floating stage in the middle of the golf course lake brought the evening to a close in a blaze of glory.

Commissioned to make headdresses for some of the most beautiful guests at these grand soirées, Paulette gave free reign to her imagination: jets of egret feathers, plumes from ostriches and birds of paradise, skullcaps decorated with sequins or gemstones, embroidered bandeaus that showed off the hair, beaded evening toques, masks of lace and organza, and brocade turbans. Silk veils of varying thicknesses, often decorated with rhinestones, were a favourite of hers – they changed the face and gave rise to pretty gestures when the wearer lifted the veil to drink or smoke.

From then on, her clients included Mrs William 'Babe' Paley and her sister Mrs John Whitney, Mrs Arturo López-Willshaw, Mrs Antenor Patiño, Mrs Jean Larivière, Princess 'Baba' de Faucigny-Lucinge, Mrs Martínez de Hoz, who came to Paulette when the House of Reboux closed, and several other of the best-dressed women in the world. Their taste for magnificence, exuberance and absolute elegance was a perfect match for Paulette's inexhaustible imagination. They had complete confidence in her. To her surprise, they would sometimes go as far as to send her their jewelry boxes so she could choose which brooches and tiaras to use on their headdresses.

Opposite: Ball at Hotel Lambert, 1950. Photograph by Robert Doisneau.

Following pages: Ball thrown by Arturo López-Willshaw at his Neuilly residence, 1952. Photograph by Robert Doisneau.

Above: The ballerina and actress Yvette Chauviré in a felt headdress with a turned-up brim embellished with peacock feathers, 1948.

Left: Venetian cornette in straw, 1948.

Opposite: Asymmetric *calot* in black velvet trimmed with pearls.

Above: The actress Renée Saint-Cyr in a large, black velvet headdress fastened with a rhinestone clip and with a jewelled veil.

Opposite: Spiral of velvet braided with grosgrain, 1949. Photograph by Horst P. Horst.

Black velvet toque topped with two small ostrich feathers and with a wide-meshed veil in brown tulle, 1951.

Paulette's fame reached as far as the Middle East. Princess Faiza of Egypt, the magnificent sister of King Farouk, ordered several designs, opening up the door to further business with the Egyptian court. The princesses of Saudi Arabia followed suit. And she still had her faithful Brazilians, Argentinians and Chileans, who took advantage of their visits to Paris to place new orders, as evoked by the novelist Nancy Mitford in her journalistic writing collated in French under the title *Une Anglaise à Paris*: 'In this area – elegance – one need look no further than a South American lady who has been dressed in Paris.'

Hats worn during the day for bridge and canasta, or for private views, appeared more restrained. They included toques worn straight on the head, fitted bonnets that revealed the forehead and felt hoods with a simple feather attached crosswise. But these hats were very carefully constructed, formed into clever shapes that sculpted the head while freeing it.

In a never-ending display of technical virtuosity, Paulette's workrooms turned out thrilling cornettes, Venetian bicornes made of fine straw, peaked *calots* made of felt or velvet, and all sorts of pointed or extended shapes with stiffened spirals, for which the milliner took inspiration from the mobiles of Alexander Calder, seeking to balance assorted volumes that appear unbalanced. The mixture of daring and rigour, the subtle finishing touches

Skullcap with horned peak, 1949.

Large asymmetric velvet, 1949.

and the preoccupation with lightness came to define the house's reputation.

Paulette counted most of European royalty and high society in general among her clients, including Isabelle, the Countess of Paris, to whom she was happy to lend hats, since the latter's means did not always permit her to buy them. No Prix de Diane or Prix du Jockey Club would have been complete without a Paulette hat on show at the weigh-in: capelines made of fine straw adorned with delicate flowers and leaves, dragonfly wings made of horsehair or starched organza, headdresses in the shape of garlands, and so on. The less wealthy

young ladies would borrow a hat from the collection for the races the following day.

Staying in the realm of the spectacular, when Paulette made hats to be worn at the theatre, they were generally modest in size so they 'did not obstruct the line of view'. Berets, toques, bonnets and skullcaps were embroidered, decorated with rhinestones, or left plain and pinned with a simple gemstone brooch. Veils were wide-meshed and rigid, or light and of double-thickness, and they were often sequined.

Turbans in graded shades of tulle, in interwoven organzas of different colours and in twill, boaters decorated

Evening headdress of coiled feathers,
1946. Photograph by Willy Maywald.

her artist's eye and sense of humour led to heart-shaped *calots* (an idea that she was to revive, thirty years later, for a Claude Montana collection), surrealist shells, and a beret resembling a ladybird complete with antennae. Her collaboration with Christian Bérard opened up new horizons, and she sometimes adapted some of her stage creations for her clients, such as the basket hats worn by the peasants in *Don Juan* and the helmet worn by Mercury in *Amphitryon*. 'The madder, the better; if not, wear a scarf,' she was fond of repeating. Nevertheless, her priority remained balance of form: adjustments had to be made by the millimetre and trimmings were secondary and never determined the inspiration behind the design.

André Lemarié, the great designer and supplier of lavish trimmings to the couture industry, recalls Paulette's highly creative, alert temperament and her innate sense of proportion. He also remembers her surprising ability to create in space: 'She was able to create something from nothing; she would crinkle up a piece of material and call her chief assistant: "Make me something like that."' Often, one of her favourite clients would ask her to make a small impromptu headdress for a soirée the next day or the day after. She would agree; she liked doing that.

with ribbons and country flowers, flat pillboxes, conical hats, close-fitting *calots*, impeccable Breton caps in felt or paillasson, casques made of multicoloured pads of pheasant feathers, velvet bicornes… None of the hats resembled another; every piece was unique.

There was no limit to Paulette's imagination: in her hands felt, straw, velvet and silk became masterpieces that were both flattering and original. Paulette allowed herself to have fun:

Opposite: Chignon-cover made from double circles of wired organza, 1960.

Left: White grosgrain sailor's beret, 1952.

Below: Black velvet 'Incroyable' headdress with a long, wide-meshed veil, 1948.

Bottom: White jersey headdress draped with eau de Nil muslin, 1950.

In general, though, Paulette's clients would choose a design from her collection. She would adjust the hat while they were wearing it, recreating it according to their face and shape. Her long, bejewelled hands would flutter, making changes with the lightest of touches, putting things in place. Paulette was adamant that the client should stand up for the final fitting so she could judge the overall effect. For her, it was not just a matter of a hat on a head: 'It is a question of legs, a way of walking; one should never try a hat on a woman who is sitting down, asking only whether the hat flatters the face.' These bespoke hats, made entirely by hand, cost between five hundred and a thousand dollars, or the price of a luxury ready-to-wear dress.

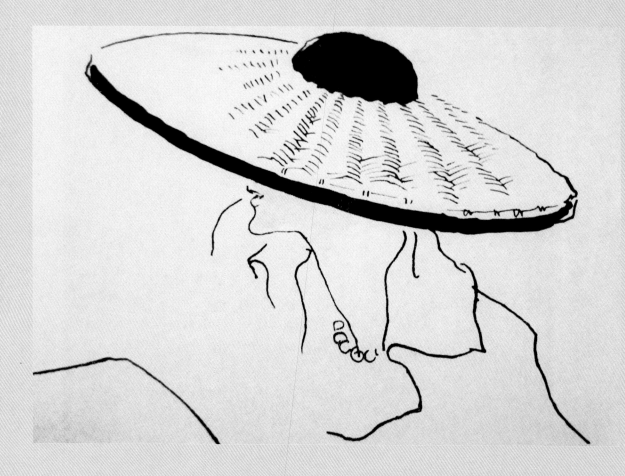

Above: Woven rush on black velvet,
1955. Illustration by Pierre Simon.

Opposite: Pillbox hat by Paulette with
a houndstooth suit in navy blue and
white by Jean Dessès, 1962.

8

America Again

aulette had divorced her first husband, who was unable to accept her success; her two sons now being older, she married Count de la Bruyère in 1951, with whom she had been engaging in a discreet love affair. He was president of the motor company Talbot and managing director of Bréguet Aviation. Through her new husband, Paulette was introduced to Protestant high society, although she did not break with her artist and designer friends, with whom the count also became friendly. His premature death in 1959 left her devastated, and she threw herself into her work more than ever, drawing on support from family and friends.

From this point on, she presented two collections per year, on 25 January and 25 July, in her salons on Avenue Franklin D. Roosevelt. Each collection contained eighty to a hundred designs. Models were dressed strictly in black to show off the hats, with their allusive names ('White

Butterfly', 'The Blue Woman', 'Black' series, 'Garibaldi', 'Velvet Eye', 'Pretty Filly', 'Bank Account').

In addition to the hundred or so hand-picked clients who were invited, there were also buyers from big American stores and their Parisian agents, as well as influential designers, such as Otto Lucas and Digby Morton from the United Kingdom and Biki – the granddaughter of Puccini – from Italy. They paid heavily for the designs, with the right to reproduce them for the ready-to-wear market. Some buyers abused this right, to the point where Parisian haute couture and *haute mode* were alarmed by the increasingly serious problem of plagiarism, to which Paulette fell victim, as did many others.

However, her fame was such that she was invited to open various shops or department-store 'corners' abroad, which went well beyond the simple purchase of designs. This was how she came to open her first shop in Buenos Aires in 1948. With salons on the first floor, it was situated on Avenida Cerrito, at the heart of the city's residential quarter, 100 metres from the French Embassy. Suzy, one of her chief assistants, was seconded there for

Black jersey cloche with a black bow and white jersey cloche with a black taffeta bandeau, designs for Saks Fifth Avenue, 1960. Photograph by William Klein.

three years and ran the whole concern, plus a workroom of eight seamstresses.

Around the same time, Paulette was invited to open a special department in Harrods in London, in which she was to present an exclusive collection. Paulette created a minimum of 250 designs a year, for her own clientele and for Harrods. Otto Lucas, the great British milliner and buyer, declared passionately that she was an 'architect of hats: you should see how they are made. From the smallest chignon-cover to the beret, the construction is unbelievable!'

She was even more successful in the United States, buoyed by the demand for luxury products and frenzied expenditure by Manhattan high society. Whether it

was dinner at a private view or cocktails at a charity gala, socialites wanted to be impeccably dressed at all times, complete with glamorous headgear. Paulette's hats were in the spotlight at the 'April in Paris Ball', which had been held in the Grand Ballroom at the Waldorf Astoria every year since 1951, in aid of the French Hospital of New York.

In 1957, the luxury department store Bergdorf Goodman, which had been buying designs from Paulette regularly since the end of the war, proposed to give her a dedicated space in its brand new millinery salon. She created twenty-five designs specially, subject to strict conditions: the hats, which were to be reproduced on site by a third party,

Opposite: Soft capeline in fine straw with an open crown rimmed with silk flowers, 1965.

Left: Purple horsehair capeline embellished with mauve anemones, created for the 'April in Paris Ball' in New York, 1953.

had to be limited in number and bear a numbered label supplied by the House of Paulette. The *haute mode* designs were to be imported directly from Paris. The same rules applied at Henri Bendel, which also planned to open a Paulette line.

Paulette received a celebrity's welcome when she walked down the steps of the Air France *Constellation*. An entire page of the *New York Herald Tribune* was dedicated to the arrival of the Countess de la Bruyère, who had just been elected president of the Chambre Syndicale de la Mode Parisienne (the milliners' union) for the next six years to bring a new impetus to this organization.

Press articles complemented her coordinated felt pillbox, recalling that she had been the pioneer of soft jersey turbans, which American women had adopted with great enthusiasm as they kept the wearer's hair in place and could be slipped into a pocket.

The 'French Collection' was presented over cocktails at Bergdorf attended by New York high society. The highlights of the collection, which was dedicated to America, were fur berets, light cloches, casques made of bright feathers, toques with feathers that trailed on the shoulders, and draped turbans.

The following year, the upmarket speciality-retail store Lord & Taylor devoted a department to Paulette's creations. In articles with the headline 'Madame Paulette of Paris', the papers

Paulette landing in New York, 1957.

her practical travelling hats, 'which keep the head warm'.

In 1959, it was the turn of Bonwit Teller to open a Paulette 'corner' in its stores in New York, Chicago, Cleveland and Boston. A year later, Saks Fifth Avenue offered her a fabulous contract, complete with a private salon on the fifth floor of the store. Twice a year, she put together a collection of sixty designs for Saks: under her supervision, the hats were then copied for ready-to-wear pieces (in a lower price range) bearing her label by a New York studio. Ernestine Carter, the high priestess of fashion journalism at the *Sunday Times*, described Paulette's 'magic touch', and there were numerous other press reports of this New York event. Paulette was surprised and amused by the avalanche of praise, and flattered to be received with great pomp by Adam Gimbel himself, president of Saks Fifth Avenue. The department store published numerous promotional inserts announcing the opening of its 'Millinery Salon' and placed a full-page advertisement in the *New York Times* on 15 September 1960 announcing its new arrival from Paris, with Paulette's photograph set beneath

quoted 'the exquisite milliner' and celebrated her flattering headgear: her small close-fitting caps and pillboxes, which she decorated with flowers, pads of feathers and mimosas; her evening headdresses made of tulle and covered with sequins to accompany the cabaret dresses and short evening frocks that were so fashionable at the time; not to mention

In her Paris studio Mme. Paulette designs for us alone the exquisite millinery bearing her label...

Mme
PAULETTE

Salon Paulette, Fifth Floor

a sheaf of tricolour flags. From this point on, around thirty employees in Paris oversaw the distribution and export to foreign branches, which Paulette visited twice a year.

Above: Advertisement for the opening of Salon Paulette at Saks Fifth Avenue, 1960.

Right: The full-page advertisement in the *New York Times*, September 1960.

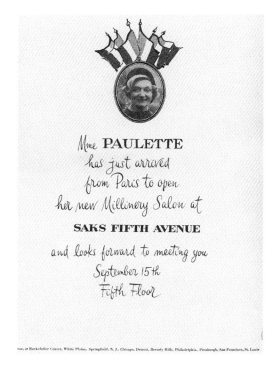

Mme **PAULETTE**
has just arrived from Paris to open her new Millinery Salon at
SAKS FIFTH AVENUE
and looks forward to meeting you September 15th Fifth Floor

roe, at Rockefeller Center, White Plains, Springfield, N. J., Chicago, Detroit, Beverly Hills, Philadelphia, Pittsburgh, San Francisco, St. Louis

Stage and Screen

Robert Piguet introduced Paulette to his group of friends, and soon they were inseparable: Jean Cocteau, Roger Vivier, Gabrielle Dorziat and Marie-Louise Bousquet, all mentioned earlier, were the central figures of the group. They were all great admirers of their friend Christian Bérard.

Prodigiously talented, this 'worldly vagabond', arbiter of all things elegant, designed enchanting sets and costumes for the theatre and ballet. The poetry of his watercolours and the freedom of his fashion sketches for *Vogue* were a reminder that he was also a great artist, whose melancholic figures haunted deserted seashores. 'Bébé', as he was known in Paris society, liked to accompany friends on shopping trips to Paulette's salons. Loquacious and kind, he would give advice, place the hat on the head with authority, move away in order to get a better look, come back to adjust it with fluttering, plump hands – he was a conjuror who made the most of his

gifts and handled everything with a surprising lightness.

In 1947, Jean-Louis Barrault and Madeleine Renaud put on Molière's *Amphitryon* at the Théâtre Marigny. While he designed the sets and costumes, Christian Bérard entrusted the hats to Paulette. She was delighted at the prospect of working with him. He explained: 'Paulette my dear, I need wonderful things. Warriors' helmets, a headdress for Night – tragic, terrifying – and feathers! A sparkling Jupiter, and a Mercury…'

'What a joy, *cher* Bébé!' she replied. 'Do you have models?'

Bérard's forget-me-not eyes narrowed in surprise.

'Models? But my dear, they're absolutely useless. Make whatever you wish. Something mad, sublime.'

He drew the outline of a helmet on a piece of paper. His hands finished off the sketch in the air.

Paulette discovered that making these helmets for the stage required a very different technique. At rehearsals, she learned to her cost that the set swallowed up small details, and that it was therefore necessary to use larger features.

The ballet *Piège de Lumière*, produced by the Marquis de Cuevas, 1951.

Costume design by Christian Bérard for
Jean-Louis Barrault in *Amphitryon*, 1947.

The last day of rehearsals was feverish, much like the run-up to a fashion show. The large hall at the Marigny was in total darkness with all the lights out. The stage curtain was taking a long time to go up. Bébé sat beside Paulette with his ears pricked for the sound of machinery moving the scenery, which should drift like clouds. He squeezed her arm nervously, attentive to every detail. He kept mopping his face, leaping up to the stage to adjust a drape, always a martyr to his obsession with perfection.

The premiere of *Amphitryon* took place on 5 December 1947. It was a triumph. Three weeks later was the premiere of *Don Juan*, directed by and starring Louis Jouvet, at the Théâtre de l'Athénée.

'How instructive for us all,' noted Paulette, 'to see an actor like Jouvet at work. Always dissatisfied with himself, he strives relentlessly for perfection. His constant doubt makes his voice flatter and more clipped. Jouvet consumes his characters; he makes them live in his place.'

Bérard's costumes were made in Robert Piguet's workrooms under the supervision of the couturier's assistant Marc Bohan, a silent, focused and passionate young man of whom Paulette was very fond. Years later, she was delighted to see him take over as creative director at Christian Dior.

The problem of helmets resolved, a more prosaic problem emerged, that of the peasants' hats for *Don Juan*, which Bérard told her should be made of braided rushes, just as they were in the country. In 1947, however, straw-workers were very conventional and could not imagine using vines or palms to make hats. At the Métro station Saint-Philippe du Roule, Paulette had noticed an elderly Italian woman repairing straw and wicker chairs. She explained to the woman that she would like a hat resembling a basket and sat down next to her to show her the shape and type of weaving.

Above: Paulette and the elderly straw-worker at
Saint-Philippe du Roule Métro, 1947.

Left: Woven rush on black velvet inspired by the
peasants' hats in *Don Juan*, 1948.

The resulting creation was completely convincing on the head of the actress Dominique Blanchar, opposite Jouvet's cruel Don Juan.

Paulette revived the idea in a simplified form for her own collection. Thus the woven rush capeline, made with the same simple technique used by the peasant women of the south, became the latest fashion at the Paris racecourses. Similarly, she brought back Mercury's helmet, as worn by Jean-Louis Barrault at the Marigny, in her Summer 1948 collection, transposing it into Neapolitan grosgrain, with the two small decorative wings adding a note of mischief and humour.

The exciting collaboration with Bérard continued with *Les Parents Terribles* in 1948, Jean Cocteau's film adaption of his own play with Paulette's great friend Gabrielle Dorziat in one of the lead roles. But this marvellous friendship with Bérard came to a sudden and dramatic end when he died of a heart attack at the age of forty-seven, leaving his friends and admirers distraught. His unique output had opened up a new and exciting field of work to Paulette that without him she would not have known.

Around the same time she met the Marquis de Cuevas, a ballet impresario who commissioned her to make numerous hair adornments for his productions of *The Sylph* (for which Bérard designed the costumes), *Petrushka*, *Piège de Lumière* and *The Blue Bird*. This new experience of the stage, which Paulette found fascinating, was yet another string to her bow, and something she was to return to in the future.

Serge Golovine in the ballet *Petrushka*, produced by the Marquis de Cuevas, 1952.

With Cecil Beaton

Paulette also had Christian Bérard to thank for introducing her to the supremely talented Cecil Beaton, who was to become a dear friend. A photographer and illustrator for *Vogue* for nearly fifty years, a writer and expert on high-society life, a connoisseur of fashion from around 1900 onwards, he was also recognized as a set designer for the London stage (he recalled being dazzled as an adolescent by the sight of the actress Gaby Deslys wearing aeroplane propeller hats: 'enormous constructions covered in exuberant feathers and tropical birds').

In 1947, the director Alexander Korda asked him to design sets and costumes for a film adaptation of Oscar Wilde's *An Ideal Husband*. Beaton had the costumes made in London, but he came to Paris specially to commission Paulette to make the twelve principal hats, based on his drawings. After doing some research, she foraged in forgotten boutiques, digging out rare types of straw and old hatpins, velvet and bobbin lace to give the hats a completely authentic late nineteenth-century appearance. She used a specialist craftsman to create exquisite varieties of flowers and to combine feathers of every kind with Italian straw and velvet.

When Beaton saw the hats, he was thrilled with the elegance of the proportions, the trimmings and the finishing touches. Paulette Goddard, the star of the film, was also delighted, despite having requested that her own ensembles be made by her habitual costume-maker in Hollywood.

Although typically British (he was the official photographer to the Royal Family), Beaton was also considered a great photographer and designer in the United States. Aware of his talent as a set and costume designer, in 1958 Vincente Minnelli asked Beaton to make the belle époque costumes for *Gigi*, the spectacular musical film he was directing based on the novel by Colette and starring Leslie Caron, Louis Jourdan and Maurice Chevalier. While helping the producer scout out filming locations in Paris, Beaton took the opportunity to

Leslie Caron in *Gigi* wearing a hat by Paulette based on drawings by Cecil Beaton, 1947. Photograph by Cecil Beaton.

109

Above: Leslie Caron in *Gigi* wearing a
large straw with a turned-up brim, 1958.
Photograph by Cecil Beaton.

Opposite: Paulette Goddard in *An Ideal
Husband* wearing the '1895' hat designed
by Paulette based on drawings by
Cecil Beaton, 1947.

invite Paulette to make the hats for Leslie and the *demi-mondaines* who frequented Maxim's in the film. The results were gardens of flowers, cascades of ribbons and ostrich feathers, and fine straws in delicate harmonies of pink, mauve and other pastels (Beaton was only too aware of the difficulty of conveying strong colours on-screen).

Paulette and Beaton were reunited six years later for what was to be the most exciting phase of their collaboration. The sumptuous costumes and improbable hats of *My Fair Lady*, a 1964 film adaptation of George Bernard Shaw's *Pygmalion* directed by George Cukor, who recreated a stylized version of Edwardian London, are as memorable today as they were fifty years ago.

Together with Paulette, Beaton dreamed up innumerable hats for Audrey Hepburn's Eliza Doolittle: large asymmetric double-sided shapes in black and white; pointed, feathered turbans; two-tone capelines with giant bows and cabbage roses; and outsize bicornes. The fitting with Audrey could not have been more compelling: she brought each design to life, with Beaton photographing her as she did so and Paulette at his side, making sure the hat was in the right place.

Finally, five or six hats were mutually agreed upon. The best known

is undoubtedly the enormous capeline tipped to one side, piled high with ostrich feathers and topped with a black-and-white-striped ribbon bow. At once graphically simple and extravagant, it rests on a delicate lace mobcap. Yet the technical feat of this hat was imperceptible and Audrey wore the elaborate edifice as gracefully as only she knew how.

Paulette continued to create hats for the French stage and screen. Her film commissions included hats for Melina Mercouri in *Promise at Dawn* (1970), Michèle Morgan in *Chéri* (1984) and Stéphane Audran in *The Blood of Others* (1984).

At the theatre, she reinvented belle époque hats for adaptations of plays by Georges Feydeau: for Madeleine Renaud in *Occupe-toi d'Amélie* (1948) and Françoise Fabian in *La Puce à l'Oreille* (1967). She was inspired by Fabian in particular, who she said had a 'head for hats', and for whom she was always happy to improvise an evening toque at the last minute. She designed a memorable veil of double thickness with square netting for the actress, who remembers Paulette as 'a *grande dame* whose style and class commanded respect'.

Opposite and next page: Audrey Hepburn in *My Fair Lady* wearing hats by Paulette based on drawings by Cecil Beaton, 1964. Photographs by Cecil Beaton.

Each new decade seemed to bring Paulette into contact with designers who captured the atmosphere of the time. In 1973, she met Groupe TSE, a theatre troupe founded and run by the Argentinian director and playwright Alfredo Arias. He was staging the revue *Luxe*, a parody of the Folies Bergère and Hollywood revues that was full of new, mad ideas and constant discrepancy and irony, at the Palace. It was love at first sight on both sides, a mutual delirium. The two designers who worked on *Luxe*, Jean-Yves Legavre and Juan Stoppani, have spoken of Paulette's 'insane talent, her loquacity, her grace and the elegance of her slender figure' (she was seventy-three at the time). Alfredo Arias, for his part, describes her as an 'incredible designer'.

It was through the Argentinian troupe that Serge Lutens came to make Paulette's acquaintance: 'Groupe TSE knew all about fashion in Paris, they knew all the right addresses.' The great creator of perfumes was at the time the artistic director at Christian Dior in charge of scents and cosmetics, and he was looking for an exceptional milliner to make the hats for his 'Venetian' publicity campaign. Paulette made some superb bicornes in violet and black for Lutens. The portrait he paints of her today is eloquent: 'She was a woman with a sense of chic, a love of life and elegance. She had *savoir faire*; she was attractive, with a certain madness, a certain fantasy. Hats for her were all about heads: she never put them on straight; she positioned them according to the wearer's face.'

Around the same time, Jean-Marie Rivière named Paulette his designer of choice for the headdresses for his revues at the cabaret L'Ange Bleu and, later, the vast music hall Le Paradis Latin. Her designs brought just the right crazy element, the refined eccentricity he was looking for.

In 1979, Paulette received a commission from the Crazy Horse Saloon, a Parisian cabaret known for its nude female dancers. The brief was so original, so improbable, so different from what she was accustomed to with her usual, more discreet clients, that she found it irresistible. Alain Bernardin, the cabaret's founder and director, asked Paulette to make modern, entertaining headdresses for the performers – for whom they were often the only item of clothing. As a 'thank you', the Crazy Horse presented Paulette with a signed photograph of Trucula Bonbon, Brandy Proforma and Bonny Chatterton, sporting a turban topped with an enormous and comical bow made of spotted satin.

By Appointment

'She made hats for the whole world.' One has only to mention the name 'Paulette' and the response is always the same. In her 1950s heyday, she had 3,500 clients, including aristocrats, wealthy members of the bourgeoisie, wives of heads of state, royalty, and stars of stage and screen. Often the actresses who met her while she was working on a play or film would return as clients in their own right, such as Audrey Hepburn, who ordered several straw pillboxes from Paulette in a rare lapse from her almost exclusive devotion to Hubert de Givenchy.

Important clients from abroad took advantage of their trips to Paris to choose designs or have a fitting. Some women, such as Greta Garbo and Marlene Dietrich, had a mould made to measure to avoid having to come in too often. Almost ceremonial in nature, fittings required four people and were not without their surprises: for example, the actress Yvonne Printemps, wife of

the playwright Sacha Guitry and then later of the actor Pierre Fresnay, was in the habit of removing her tight-fitting jacket to try on a hat with a bare torso.

Eva Perón was a regular client of the shop in Buenos Aires, where Suzy attended to her personally, but she still paid a visit to Paulette during her official visit to Paris in 1947.

It was not unusual for famous clients to turn up in Paris from one of the four corners of the globe without an appointment. This could make it difficult to avoid faux pas and to manage hostilities. For example, the mother of President John F. Kennedy, Rose Kennedy, with whom Paulette enjoyed a long-lasting friendship, was on no account to find herself in the same room as Gloria Swanson, her husband's former official mistress.

In 1949, Rita Hayworth, whom Paulette liked dressing in 'garden party' capelines, married Aly Khan wearing a light hat of sky-blue organdie that matched her dress by Jacques Fath. This type of capeline was also popular with the sisters of King Farouk of Egypt, who were splendid beauties. Princess Fawzia, whose

Paulette trying a large capeline on Rita Hayworth, 1948. Photograph by Willy Rizzo.

first husband was the Shah of Iran, and her sister Faiza bought their clothes in Paris and were clients of Paulette. At their request, she organized a presentation of her collection over tea at the Semiramis Hotel in Cairo, on house models who had come from Paris. It was a great success with the ladies of the court. Two months later in May 1951, Paulette and her team returned to Cairo for the wedding of King Farouk and Narriman Sadek. Farouk was determined to entrust the fitting of the new queen's tiara and veil to Paulette and he was present throughout.

However, adding the finishing touches to numerous hats ordered by the royal entourage began to slow Paulette down and she became anxious. Without hesitating, the king gave the order that her train must wait for her, to the great exasperation of the other travellers.

Princess Soraya of Iran ordered multiple hats from Paulette each time she visited Paris. Paulette steered her towards small hats without a veil that showed off her magnificent green eyes. Later, Empress Farah of Iran was to sport even more daring hats, in keeping with her Parisian elegance. She was to remain a faithful customer until the closure of the House of Paulette. Princess Paola of Belgium chose turbans that showed

off the perfect oval of her face. Princess Grace of Monaco, to whom Marc Bohan and the famous hair stylist Alexandre had recommended Paulette, was also a fan of the practical turban.

With the big international film stars, everything was, of course, more complicated. The ever-professional Marlene Dietrich knew exactly what suited the shape of her face. She was demanding and precise, and her collection of hats and fur toques (which she kept for a long time) was impressive.

For Greta Garbo, who shunned publicity following her early retirement, cloches and hats with turned-down brims were the order of the day as they enabled her to hide her face. Garbo would visit Paulette's salons after the other clients and staff had left. She appreciated the lightness and comfort of Paulette's creations and chose designs of the greatest apparent simplicity. Still, this did not prevent her from mixing her *haute mode* hats, complete with their invisible refinements, with everyday straws bought on impulse while on her travels.

Gloria Swanson chez Paulette for a turban fitting, 1968.

Above: Princess Soraya of Iran and
Shah Muhammad Reza Pahlavi,
1955.

Opposite: Princess Faiza of Egypt,
sister of King Farouk, wearing a large
rigid straw capeline, 1946.

In general, though, film actresses were rather intimidated and easy to advise, and not always sure of themselves. Monarchs also had absolute confidence in their milliner, who travelled to their respective residences in order to show them her designs and take their measurements. Demure berets and small headdresses for the queens of Greece, Norway and Sweden; capelines for grand occasions for the Queen of Jordan and the Duchess of Kent, to whom Paulette had been recommended by Cecil Beaton. The latter favoured small toques and boaters that showed off her fine face, as the protocol required.

The perfect manners of Pauline de la Bruyère (who never mentioned her title), her discretion and her ease of bearing when dealing with powerful people were undeniable assets in her building up and retaining a fashionable and aristocratic clientele from around the world.

Opposite: Hairnet embellished with small, white flowers fashioned by hand, 1966.

Above: Empress Farah of Iran sporting a similar model, 1966.

Left: Princess Paola of Belgium, wearing an organza turban in pink and green, 1962.

Opposite: Lilian, Princesse de Réthy, in a
leopard-skin toque, with the former King
Leopold III of Belgium, 1962.

Above: The forever-elegant Marlene Dietrich
in a soft felt hat with a silk headband, 1965.

The majestic Begum Aga Khan III was a loyal client who acquired turbans and untrimmed capelines for her numerous appearances in the stands at the races. Baroness Marie-Hélène de Rothschild, on the other hand, went for capelines that were weighed down with fruit, flowers and feathers; she knew how to wear them joyfully and provocatively.

In 1970, Madame Georges Pompidou asked Paulette, her milliner for the past ten years, to solve the problem of hats for her official visit to the United States (hats were still wardrobe essentials for American women at the time). Three cloches, three mink toques, plus a number of capelines and evening bandeaus were produced as a matter of urgency.

As official milliner to the wife of the President of the Republic, Paulette provided Anne-Aymone Giscard d'Estaing with discreet flat toques with short veils, small straw cloches, chignon-covers made of flower petals and a large quantity of other charming headdresses, which the first lady later presented to the Musée Galliera. Although Bernadette Chirac wore hats less often, she did not hesitate to call on Paulette for various formal events.

Paulette continued to make hats for all kinds of fashionable and society occasions, for women who were considered among the best dressed in the world: Patricia López-Willshaw, Evangeline Bruce (the famous wife of the American diplomat David Bruce), Lolly Larivière, Madame Ortiz-Linarès, Lady Abdy, Laís Carvalho Araújo, Lady Deterding, Francine Weisweiller, Ghislaine de Polignac and Beatriz Patiño, who, on each of her trips to Paris, added three mourning hats to her order, 'just in case'.

Babe Paley, one of Truman Capote's famous 'swans' (glamorous Manhattan socialites) and the absolute queen of New York high society, and Vicomtesse Jacqueline de Ribes, who was crowned 'the most elegant woman in the world', appreciated the way Paulette showed off their beauty; a photograph of the very aristocratic Vicomtesse wearing a sable and white karakul toque was taken up by the entire international fashion press. Fiona Campbell-Walter was also very beautiful: once an occasional model for Paulette, she became a client after her marriage to Baron Thyssen-Bornemisza.

The Vicomtesse de Ribes wearing a sable toque with a white crown of karakul's pelt during the preparations for the Embassy Ball, 1959. Photograph by Snowdon.

President Georges Pompidou
and his wife, Claude, on an
official visit, 1962.

The Begum Aga Khan III at the
Prix de Diane at Chantilly, 1957.

Paulette's dealings with the Duchess of Windsor, who was particular, narcissistic and complicated, were more delicate. The duke would join her for fittings, waiting quietly in a separate salon. On the day of his funeral in 1972, Paulette came to the villa in the Bois de Boulogne to drape the mourning veil over Wallis; she could not fail to be surprised by the attitude of the duchess, who spent a good ten minutes modifying the arrangement so her face was in the light. She was to leave this organza veil of remarkable proportions to the Windsor Museum in her will.

The most surprising client among this 'who's who' of famous women is undeniably Imelda Marcos. There is no doubt that the Philippine dictator's wife's collection of hats was not as large as her collection of shoes, but there was no limit to her spending sprees – hence a caricature in an American newspaper that showed boxes signed 'Paulette' in the middle of what could be called the spoils of war.

There were other women, too, who counted among her favourite clients: the young Catherine Rivière, for example, the wife of the director of L'Ange Bleu and Le Paradis Latin, whose facial structure, eyes and lips were reminiscent of Garbo; she inspired Paulette, who accentuated her style with jersey turbans, cloches with turned-up brims, and trilbies with pheasant feathers and frothy veils, adding a dose of glamour to the overall effect.

Certainly less Hollywood but just as unconditional an admirer of Paulette was the artist Sonia Delaunay, who became a friend after being introduced by Roger Vivier. Fashion still interested Delaunay, who designed fabrics and had even opened a textile shop before the war. Now carrying a little extra weight, but still cinched into the same navy blue suits, she never missed presentations of her friend's collections, and Paulette took on board her insightful comments. They dined together regularly: at Paulette's apartment on Place d'Iéna or her countryside home at Grosrouvre (with Sonia never failing to bring along her habitual salmon coulibiac), or at Sonia's studio on Rue de Saint-Simon.

Such was Paulette's reputation for impeccable taste that the great British florist Constance Spry asked her to put together a traditional French bouquet to feature in one of her books on flower arrangement. Extremely flattered, Paulette surpassed herself, creating a large, balanced, triangular bouquet in the spirit of the seventeenth century.

Queen Elizabeth II, the Duchess of Windsor and Queen Elizabeth, the Queen Mother at the funeral of the Duke of Windsor, June 1972.

Imelda Marcos leaving for exile with her vast collection
of designer clothes, shoes and accessories, including a
hat box labelled 'Paulette', 1986.

The Begum Aga Khan III and Bettina Graziani at the
Longchamp races, 1958.

End of an Era

In 1955, Paulette was the reigning queen of *haute mode*, with 3,500 clients, some from as far afield as Canada and Australia. Film stars and royalty came incognito for their fittings in her small salon. For these hardy travellers, she even had made a light valise suitable for transporting four hats.

The 1960s marked the end of this golden age. The fashion for backcombed and puffed-up hairstyles made hat-wearing impossible, at the same time as the social significance of such accessories as gloves and hats disappeared. In the fashion magazines, the creations of hair stylists replaced those of milliners. Brigitte Bardot's beehive had devastating effects: Parisians began to appear bare-headed in public, regardless of their age, hair blowing freely in the wind. Paulette deplored this negligence, which she compared unfavourably to the neatly hatted and faultless appearance of the Americans. As far as she was concerned, it was the idea of elegance itself that was at stake.

Jean Shrimpton wearing a black horsehair capeline 'veiled' with a soft net capeline, 1963. Photograph by John French.

The couturiers also resented this radical change in society. As president of the Chambre Syndicale de la Mode Parisienne, Paulette went on the offensive, organizing promotional shows that brought together the press, buyers and major clients. An event held at the Eiffel Tower in July 1960 caused a sensation, and resulted in Paulette being awarded the '*Prix du Tout-Paris*', to which the American journalist Art Buchwald devoted a long article.

Under Paulette's leadership, Parisian milliners organized all sorts of in situ displays of pretty young ladies wearing hats, sitting on the terraces of the cafés along the Champs-Elysées, in an attempt to re-interest women in *haute mode*.

In spite of these efforts, however, the millinery houses closed one after another. Paulette's widespread fame protected her, and she was to continue to present her collections of sixty designs twice a year for the next twenty years, but she was alone. Major foreign buyers continued to fill her order books on a regular basis. Although they no longer wore as many hats, French clients still turned to Paulette for grand occasions, gala evenings and

Beige veiled velvet decorated with
two woollen pompoms, 1963.

weddings. Bridal headdresses had become one of her specialities: she knew better than anyone how to arrange clouds of tulle, and to bring imagination to the designs.

Paulette was more creative than ever, reinventing traditional forms and using materials that did not usually feature in *haute mode*: plastic-coated raffia, celluloid and even denim. Once again, she put all her expertise to work in crafting turbans: jersey creations with long scarves, designs that tied at the back, as well as forms made of chenille, draped tulle or different-coloured organza.

The capelines were simple and light, made mostly of horsehair or wired tulle. Straw hats with wide, turned-up brims were still in vogue, but Paulette had practically abandoned her precious veils. Now, lines were clean and faces uncovered: *trotteurs* (snug-fitting cloches), Breton caps, felt cloches, plain skullcaps, thick pillboxes made of fine straw or paillasson, hoods and melon hats (her famous bowlers) accompanied coats and suits. Bowl-shaped hats worn on hair tied back and cloches with high crowns were matched with clothes and often came without trimmings.

Around the same time, Paulette began a collaboration with the Revillon and Chombert fur companies. The success of

Left: Velvet hat and silk veil with *point d'esprit* stitching, 1961.

Right: Veiled toque mounted with a nest of leaves, 1961.

the 1965 film *Doctor Zhivago* inspired her to create toques made of sumptuous fur – sable, chinchilla, fox – with an emphasis on shapes that were anything but banal. She made bowler hats, pillboxes, cloches and caps made of ocelot and panther. Mink worked well with capelines, bonnets and large berets.

Her imagination defied the new constraints: she dreamed up Bersaglieri hats with crests of cockerel feathers, close-fitting casques with small, pasted pheasant feathers, and *calots* decorated with large metal studs or embroidered with swirls of topaz. In 1966, her '*cages à cheveux*' ('hair cages'), made of transparent plastic and photographed by Raymond Depardon, caused a sensation, as did her veil with two painted red cheeks, one of her nods to surrealism.

Paulette also played with images of an exquisite femininity by developing her use of fabric flowers that had been shaped with an iron and sewn one by one onto tulle mesh. There were close-fitting toques made of minuscule lilac flowers, toques made of lily of the valley or camellias with green leaves, toques made of leaves, cloches covered entirely in anemones and even a poisonous bush of red poppies on black tulle.

Grand balls became few and far between. Hélène Rochas's ball at La Grande Cascade in the Bois de Boulogne in 1965, which took *My Fair Lady* as its theme and was attended by Cecil Beaton,

Two-coloured felt beret, 1960.

was a high point for Paulette, who had made Audrey Hepburn's spectacular hats for the film. She recreated capelines and other extravagant shapes with plenty of feathers and ribbons for several of the guests. In 1969, Baron Alexis de Rédé held his unforgettable '*Bal Oriental*' at the Hotel Lambert on Ile Saint-Louis; Paulette came up with a number of refined edifices of feathers and ornamental gemstones on top of sultans' turbans made of brocade or mousseline, which fitted with the atmosphere of *A Thousand and One Nights*.

In 1971 and 1972, it was the turn of Marie-Hélène de Rothschild to stage two memorable events at Château de Ferrières: the '*Bal Proust*' and the '*Bal Surréaliste*' were attended by all of international high society and gave Paulette the opportunity to invent more fabulous headdresses for numerous guests.

These were to be the last big private events in Paris. From then on, evenings out often had a commercial purpose and were organized to launch luxury products or to mark official openings.

Above: Ocelot bowler, 1961.

Left: Felt *calot* with layered golden fringing, 1962.

Paulette had been working in collaboration with the hair stylist Alexandre for a while, to put an end to the war between hair and hats. For him, she designed chignon-covers and other light headdresses that left hairstyles intact: horsehair swirls, simple veil bandeaus decorated with rhinestones or cloches of meshed veil.

As far as her own collections of chignon-covers and bandeaus were concerned, she was as imaginative as ever, playing with ostrich feathers, cherries, flowers and gold lamé. Her bonnets worn tipped forward over the forehead and plumed at the back went some way to reconciling young women to hats.

Left: Pointed hat covered with flowers in varying shades of blue, 1962.

Right: Blue satin *calot* covered with silk hortensia petals, 1962.

Opposite: Close-fitting toque with shocking-pink rose petals, 1964.

Right: Black velvet chignon-
cover with two ostrich-feather
pompoms, 1965.

Opposite: Cascade of petals
in black organza, 1965.

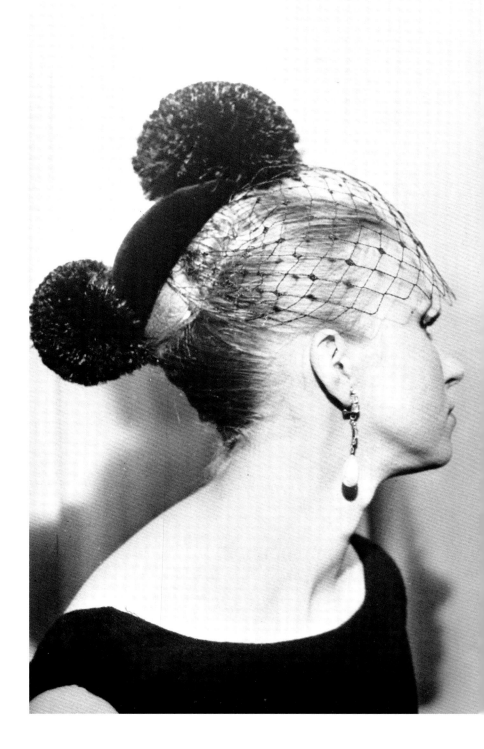

For grand occasions, women were fond of capelines laden with large silk flowers that could be worn with long hair.

Her famous clients – notably Americans – were as faithful as ever; she was the official milliner to successive wives of the President of the French Republic; and the couturiers continued to invite her to design hats for their catwalk shows. Her impeccable creativity was also in demand from theatre and music hall costumiers seeking headdresses for the stage. In 1980, she still had five hundred clients. But the business was now costing her a great deal of money, and she was eventually forced to merge her workrooms and salons into a single floor at 63 Avenue Franklin D. Roosevelt.

Yet she refused to stop working and declared: 'The hat is my dancer, the *bibi* my tutu.' She entered into a collaboration with the two most avant-garde young ready-to-wear designers of the day: Claude Montana and Thierry Mugler. Despite being more than eighty years old, she would still amaze them.

Illustration from *The Snob-Spotter's Guide* by Philippe Jullian, 1958.

Straw chignon-cover topped with
ostrich feathers, 1966.

Above: Green-and-blue ostrich-feather
wig, Spring/Summer 1968.

Opposite: Red-and-white fox hood,
Autumn/Winter 1965.

13

The Couture Houses

Robert Piguet was the first couturier to use an official external milliner. He appreciated the quality of Paulette's designs and above all the richness of her imagination. During the ten years of their collaboration (he retired from haute couture in 1951 for health reasons), Piguet maintained a deep friendship with his beloved *modiste*. For each of his collections, Paulette made hats that matched perfectly the dresses and suits that they accompanied or enhanced them with a hint of eccentricity.

These were favourite topics of conversation for this master of elegance, whose assistants included Christian Dior, Pierre Balmain, Antonio del Castillo, Hubert de Givenchy and Marc Bohan. Sensitive to the cold, he was always wrapped in a large mink-lined coat and driven in a black Hispano-Suiza by a chauffeur wearing livery.

Piguet was such a devoted friend of Paulette's that he bought a house, which he called '*La Voisine*' ('the neighbour'), just 100 metres from her property at Grosrouvre in the Ile-de-France region.

It was only with the closure of Maison Piguet in July 1951 that Paulette agreed to work for other couturiers. They all recognized her as hugely influential. Some allowed her to sign her hats; others preferred to label them with their own name. Paulette was not offended: for her, the main thing was to create, to allow herself to be stimulated by the different environments, to find the correct response to the couturiers' (sometimes vague) wishes and to surprise them.

Most of Madame Grès's turbans were made by Paulette. She collaborated occasionally with Paquin, Pierre Balmain, Pierre Cardin, Jacques Heim and many others. On the other hand, she put together collection after collection for Jean Dessès, Jacques Griffe, Jeanne Lafaurie, Hanae Mori, Louis Féraud, Guy Laroche and Emanuel Ungaro, for whom in the mid-1960s she created plain close-fitting toques to match coats; bowl-shaped hats made of fur, woollen fabric, jersey and canvas; plus fur berets, trilbies with chin straps, pillboxes, kerchiefs, Egyptian toques and bonnets of all kinds.

Robert Piguet, 1948.

Top row:
Collection Montana,
Winter 1982/83

Left: The four aces.

Centre: Lined up, the black
letters on the felt toques spell
out 'Montana'.

Right: Headdresses made
from sequined cut-outs of two
crossed hands.

Bottom row:
Collection Montana,
Winter 1983/84

Left and centre: A cascade of
tulle erupts from the bride's
rhinestone headpiece.

Right: Vaporous veils envelop
passers-by on the 'Twilight
Boulevard'.

Even when the couture houses had their own hat ateliers, clients often preferred to go to Paulette. A ready-made hat might complement the line of a garment perfectly at a fashion show, but it could not compete with a made-to-measure piece by a great *modiste*, as even some couturiers admitted. A master milliner would consider the proportion of shapes with respect to a woman's face and adjust the hat exactly to the contours of her head, prioritizing comfort as well as paying close attention to the minutiae of finishings and offering a choice of fabrics and trimmings.

Christian Dior, for one, was sometimes sorry not to be able to call on Paulette for an original creation without displeasing his hat atelier, which was under the management of his muse and collaborator Mitzah Bricard. Nevertheless, this did not prevent him from paying frequent visits to Place d'Iéna to play patience with his dear friend over tea, accompanied by his little dog.

When she closed her hat atelier in 1971, Mademoiselle Chanel, a former milliner herself, asked Paulette to make fabric boaters and small tweed Breton caps. When Karl Lagerfeld took over as chief designer for Chanel in 1983, he spontaneously called on Paulette for his haute couture collection, asking her to

Men's trilby in felt for Jean-Louis Scherrer, Winter 1978.

design 'fontanges' (tall headdresses that were à la mode in the court of Louis XIV) to be worn with evening dresses.

When Paulette passed away eighteen months later, Lagerfeld paid her the following tribute: 'She was the last in a line of this kind of artist. She had something in her fingers, a magic touch, a scientific understanding of the drape of a turban, for example. Nowadays, lots of people know how to make charming, simple hats, but it's not the same thing.'

As she had done long before with Robert Piguet, Paulette established a friendly and exclusive working relationship with Jean-Louis Scherrer: for more than ten years, she made the hats for all his collections. The couturier provided her with a quick sketch of volumes and fabric samples for colours.

Then her imagination took over.
The results were always overwhelmingly elegant yet totally modern, and sometimes with unusual trimmings: from the extreme chic of a sporty trilby or a simple beret covered in studs, to unexpected gold embroidery, a maharani's turban in lamé or a veil topped off with a jewel. At the rehearsals for Scherrer's shows, Paulette would stand to the left of the couturier, attentive and precise as she scrutinized each hat for imperfections. The strange wicker basket that she carried around with her from one rehearsal to the next contained trimmings of all kinds to add a finishing touch to a trilby or a boater. Scherrer had such confidence in her taste that he did not hesitate to ask her opinion on a dress or suit. As for Paulette, she was perfectly at ease in this elegant and civilized couture house, where she was revered.

Paulette continued to show her collections twice a year. She was to experience one last triumph, in the most unexpected way, with the two star ready-to-wear designers of the 1980s, who brought her in to add to the theatricality of their spectacular shows. She enjoyed pandering to Thierry Mugler's visionary fantasies: skullcaps embroidered with insects, catwoman masks, bandeaus with rigid, vertical shells or large velvet rolls,

Puss in Boots-style hats, horsehair swirls, dragonflies made of coloured organza for flower women, and so on.

With Claude Montana, Paulette gave free rein to her artistic temperament. As he states simply: 'I thought my message was incomplete without hats, so I gave Paulette guidelines for each look and she interpreted them.' What was to follow were some of the most dazzling hats Paulette ever made. In the final tricolour look of the Winter 1978/79 collection, the bride wore red; her feathered headpiece, edged with rhinestones and ruby-coloured cabochons, was topped with two wings holding in place a veil of red tulle. For the Winter 1982/83 collection, there were headdresses sculpted in relief portraying the four aces of a pack of cards for a red-and-black look, two black-and-white hands folded on the forehead with pink-sequined nails, black letters spelling the name 'Montana' when the models lined up and *calots* topped with three tennis balls.

For the Winter 1983/84 collection, Paulette revisited men's trilbies, bandeaus with sculpted peaks, cut-out helms made of organza, spiral bonnets tilted forwards and skullcaps with extravagant geometric

Paulette, 1980. Photograph by Helmut Newton.

cut-outs. Cascades of sable and gold tulle escaped from sequined headpieces and faces were enveloped in vaporous veils for a look called 'Twilight Boulevard'. Finally came a sublime bride, whose rhinestone headpiece in the shape of a heart released streams of tulle veined with more rhinestones. It was a surprising final fireworks display that Paulette could not know was to be her last.

Indeed, Paulette was not to attend the presentation of the next collection, for which she had finished the hats a few days previously. She died suddenly, on 8 September 1984. At the age of eighty-four, she was still full of humour and audacity, and possessed of an inexhaustible imagination.

Among many others, the newspaper *Libération* paid her tribute: 'There was in every hat by Madame Paulette – in the drape of a jersey turban, the volume of a fur toque, the impeccable line of a simple Breton cap, the lightness of a horsehair capeline, the skilful structure of flowers and stones of one of her evening toques – the inimitable allure and grace of a great lady who must once have been very beautiful, and who retained until the end, with her sparkling, mischievous eyes, a fascinating charm.'

When she looked back over her career, Paulette recognized that although it had involved heavy constraints and demanded constant energy, it had enabled her to forge close relationships and to meet unusual people, whose originality and friendship she appreciated.

Nevertheless, she did not sacrifice her personal life to her career, as is so often the case. She delighted in gathering her sons' families and her friends around large joyful dinner tables every weekend. She also put her considerable talents as a landscaper to good use at her property at Grosrouvre, a dilapidated sheep barn she bought in 1947 that became a superb country residence.

A few months after her sudden death, the Musée Galliera, a fashion museum in Paris, organized a tribute exhibition in her memory entitled 'Coup de chapeau à Madame Paulette' ('Hats off to Madame Paulette'). The invitation to the opening asked women to wear hats in memory of the great milliner.

Today, the Musée Galliera has in its collection around one hundred of her creations, donated by clients. A further hundred or so have been bequeathed to the Musée des Arts Décoratifs. There are also several museums outside France that have Paulette hats in their collections, notably the Costume Institute at the Metropolitan Museum of Art and the Museum of the City of New York.

Acknowledgments

The author is grateful to have been able to rely on the family archives, as well as on contemporary reports in French and American newspapers and magazines.

For their invaluable assistance in her research, she would like to thank: Alfredo Arias, Vanessa Bernard, Marc Bohan, Eliane Bolomier, Sandrine Bourg, Marie-Louise de Clermont-Tonnerre, Oriole Cullen, Claudine Delbard, Josette Desnus, Denise Dubois, Olivier Echaudemaison, Fabienne Faluel, Brigitte Govignon, Bettina Graziani, Thomas M. Gunther, Marie-Laure Gutton, Stephen Jones, Sylvie Lecallier, Jean-Yves Legavre and Juan Stoppani, André Lemarié, Serge Lutens, Raymond Massaro, Claude Montana, Claudia Niedzielski, Jutta Niemann, Béatrice Paul, Bertrand Pizzin, Marie-Hélène Poix, Lorenzo Ré, Jacqueline de Ribes, Catherine Rivière, Eve Ruggieri, Jean-Louis Scherrer, Susan Train, Dominique Versavel, Alexandre Zouari and the Zahm Collection.

She would also like to express her gratitude to the following people, without whom this book would have never been possible: Thomas Neurath and Philip Watson at Thames & Hudson, and Olivier Daulte at La Bibliothèque des Arts.

The initial layout was designed by Charles Ameline and Marylène Lhenri, and completed by Lauren Necati at Thames & Hudson.

Finally, she would like to dedicate this book to Jacques Marchand, Madame Paulette's second son.

Further Reading

André Ostier: Photographies. Paris: Fondation Pierre Bergé Yves Saint Laurent, 2006. Exh. cat.

Aubenas, Sylvie, and Xavier Demange, *Elegance: The Seeberger Brothers and the Birth of Fashion Photography*. New York: Chronicle, 2007.

Baudot, François, *Fashion: The Twentieth Century*. New York: Universe, 1999.

Bolomier, Eliane, 'Le chapelier et la modiste', in *Les Artisans de l'élégance*. Paris: RMN, 1993.

——, *Le Chapeau: Grand art et savoir-faire*. Paris: Musée du Chapeau and Somogy éditions d'art, 1996.

Bolomier, Eliane, et al., *Encyclopédie du couvre-chef*. Paris: Samedi Midi Editions, 2008.

Beaton, Sir Cecil, *Cinquante ans d'élégance et d'art de vivre*. Paris: Amiot-Dumont, 1954.

——, *Cecil Beaton: 50 ans de collaboration avec Vogue*. Paris: Herscher, 1986.

Bony, Anne, *Les années 50*. Paris: Editions du Regard, 1982.

——, *Les années 60*. Paris: Editions du Regard, 1983.

——, *Les années 70*. Paris: Editions du Regard, 1993.

Delbourg-Delphis, Marylène, *Le chic et le look: Histoire de la mode féminine et des mœurs, de 1850 à nos jours*. Paris: Hachette, 1981.

Demornex, Jacqueline, *Le siècle en chapeaux: Claude Saint-Cyr: Histoire d'une modiste*. Paris: Du May, 1998.

Deslandres, Yvonne, and Florence Müller, *Histoire de la Mode au XXe siècle*. Paris: Somogy éditions d'art, 1986.

D'Orleans, Francis, *Snob Society*. Paris: Flammarion, 2009.

Dior, Christian, *Dior by Dior: The Autobiography of Christian Dior*. London: V&A Publishing, 2007.

Falluel, Fabienne, and Marie-Laure Gutton, *Elégance et Système D: Paris 1940–1944*. Paris Musées Editions, 2009.

Faucigny-Lucinge, Jean-Louis de, *Legendary Parties: 1922–1972*. New York: Vendome Press, 1987.

Ginsburg, Madeleine, *The Hat*. London: Studio Editions, 1990.

Jullian, Philippe, *The Snob Spotter's Guide*. London: Weidenfeld & Nicolson, 1958.

——, *Café-Society*. Paris: Albin Michel, 1962.

Le Maux, Nicole, *Histoire du chapeau féminin*. Paris: Charles Massin, 2000.

McDowell, Colin, *Hats: Status, Style, Glamour*. London: Thames & Hudson, 1997.

Mercié, Marie, and Sophie-Charlotte Capdevielle, *Voyage autour d'un chapeau*. Paris: Ramsay, 1990.

Müller, Florence, and Lydia Kamitsis, *Les chapeaux: Une histoire de tête*. Paris: Syro Alternatives, 1993.

O'Hara Callan, Georgina, *The Thames & Hudson Dictionary of Fashion and Fashion Designers*. London: Thames & Hudson, 2008.

Remaury, Bruno, *Dictionnaire de la Mode du XXème siècle*. Paris: Editions du Regard, 1994.

Rochas, Michel, *Vingt-cinq ans d'élégance à Paris: 1925–1950*. Paris: Pierre Tisné, 1951.

Shields, Jody, *Hats: A Stylish History and Collector's Guide*. New York: Clarkson Potter, 1991.

Steele, Valerie, *Paris Fashion: A Cultural History*. Oxford: Berg, 1988.

——, *Se vêtir au 20e siècle: De 1945 à nos jours*. Paris: Adam Biro, 1998.

Terras, Lucien, and Tristan Tzara, *L'Histoire du chapeau*. Paris: J. Damase, 1987.

Train, Susan, et al., *Le Théâtre de la Mode*. New York: Rizzoli, 1991.

Veillon, Dominique, *Fashion Under the Occupation*. Oxford: Berg, 2002.

Walford, Jonathan, *Forties Fashion: From Siren Suits to the New Look*. London: Thames & Hudson, 2008.

Illustration Credits

Index

Page numbers in *italic* refer to illustrations.

Aga Khan III, Begum 13, 128, *131*, *135*
Agnès 21, 26
Aimée, Anouk *52*
Albouy, Gérard 11, 26
Alexandre 120, 142
Amphitryon 13, 92, 103–4, *104*
L'Ange Bleu, Paris 115, 133
Arias, Alfredo 115
L'Art et la Mode 35, 42
Avedon, Richard 13, *15*, *43*, 68

Balenciaga, Cristóbal 42, 70
Balmain, Pierre 42, 151
Barbosa, Helena Ruy 25
Bardot, Brigitte 137
Barrault, Jean-Louis 44, 103, *104*, 107
Beaton, Cecil 13, 44, *108*, 109–15, 140
Beauvoir, Simone de 41
Beistegui, Carlos de 83
Bérard, Christian 13, 31, 44, 51, *54*, 75, 92, 103–4, *104*, 107, 109
Bergdorf Goodman, New York 98, 99
Biki 97
Bohan, Marc 104, 120, 151
Bonwit Teller 100
Bourdin, Guy 13
Bousquet, Marie-Louise 75, 103
Brandt, Bill *72*
Brenot, Pierre-Laurent *46*
Bricard, Mitzah 153
Brunet et Verlaine 22, 25
Bruyère *32*
Bruyère, Count de la 97
Buchwald, Art 137

Calder, Alexander 76, 89
Campbell-Walter, Fiona 128
Capote, Truman 128
Cardin, Pierre 151
Caron, Leslie *108*, 109, *111*, 112
Carter, Ernestine 100
Chambre Syndicale de la Haute Couture 33, 47, 51
Chambre Syndicale de la Mode Parisienne 99, 137
Chanel, Coco 42, 153
Chevalier, Maurice 22, 109
Chirac, Bernadette 128
Clarke, Henry 13, *59*
Cocteau, Jean 13, 44, 51, 103, 107
Crazy Horse Saloon, Paris 115
Cuevas, Marquis de 83, *102*, *106*, 107

Daniels, Elise *43*
Delaunay, Sonia 133
Delfau, André *32*

Demachy, Jacques *28*, *58*, *80*
Dessès, Jean *95*, 151
Dietrich, Marlene 13, 69, 119, 120, *127*
Dignimont, André *48–49*, 51
Dior, Christian 41, 42, 79, 151, 153; house of 9, 11, 104, 115
Doisneau, Robert *82*, *84–85*
Don Juan 13, 92, 104, *105*
Dondel, Jean-Claude *30*, 31
Dorziat, Gabrielle 44, 103, 107
Duchamp, Marcel 76

Elizabeth II, Queen 26, *132*
Elle 70

Fabian, Françoise 112
Faiza of Egypt, Princess 89, 120, *122*
Farah of Iran, Empress 120, *125*
Farouk I of Egypt, King 89, 119–20, 123
Fath, Jacques 42, 119
Fawzia of Egypt, Princess 119–20
Feydeau, Georges 112
Folies Bergère, Paris 22, 115
Ford II, Mrs Henry 64
French, John *136*
Fromentin 64

Garbo, Greta 13, 119, 120, 133
Gigi 13, *108*, 109, *111*
Gimbel, Adam 100
Giscard d'Estaing, Anne-Aymone 128
Givenchy, Hubert de 119, 151
Goddard, Paulette 109, *110*
Golovine, Serge *106*
Grace of Monaco, Princess 10, 13, 120
Graziani, Bettina *135*
Grès 42, 151
Griffe, Jacques 151
Groupe TSE 115
Gruau, René *81*

Harcourt *12*
Harper's Bazaar 10, 13, 75
Harrods, London 98
Hartnell, Norman 26
Hayworth, Rita 13, *118*, 119
Heim, Jacques 151
Henri Bendel, New York 99
Hepburn, Audrey 13, 112, *113*, *114*, 119, 141
Horst, Horst P. 13, *77*, *89*

An Ideal Husband 13, 109, *110*
Isabelle, Countess of Paris 90

Jourdan, Louis 109
Jouvet, Louis 104, 107
Jullian, Philippe 75, *146*

Kennedy, Jackie 55
Kennedy, John F. 119
Kennedy, Rose 13, 119
Khan, Aly 119
Klein, William 13, *96*
Kochno, Boris 51
Korda, Alexander 109

Lagerfeld, Karl 153
Lanvin, Jeanne 42
Larivière, Lolly 83, 128
Laroche, Guy 151
Léger, Fernand 76
Legeron 64
Legroux Sœurs 26
Leigh, Dorian 15
Lelong, Lucien 33, 41, 42
Lemarié, André 64, 92
Leopold III of Belgium, King 126
Lilian, Princess of Réthy 126
López-Willshaw, Arturo *82*
López-Willshaw, Patricia 83, 128
Lord & Taylor, New York 99
Louchel, Pierre *54*
Lucas, Otto 56, 97, 98
Lutens, Serge 115
Luxe 115

Mainbocher 42
Maison Lewis *20*, 21, *23*
Marchand, Raymond 22, *22*
Marcos, Imelda 133, *134*
Martins, Carlos 26, 31, 76
Martins, Maria 26, 31, 76
Maxim's, Paris 36, 79, *81*, 112
Maywald, Willy *8*, *52*, *53*, *91*
Metropolitan Museum of Art, New York 55, 156
Minnelli, Vincente 109
Mitford, Nancy 89
Montana, Claude 9, 15, 92, 146, 154
Mori, Hanae 151
Morton, Digby 97
Mourgue, Pierre *80*
Mugler, Thierry 10, 14, 146, 154
Musée des Arts Décoratifs, Paris *48–49*, *50*, 51, 156
Musée Galliera, Paris 128, 156
Museum of the City of New York 156
My Fair Lady 13, 112, *113*, *114*, 140–41

Nepo, Arik *78*
Newton, Helmut 13, *155*

L'Officiel de la Couture 9, 42

Pahlavi, Shah Muhammad Reza 120, *123*
Paley, Mrs William 'Babe' 83, 128

Paola of Belgium, Princess 13, 120, *125*
Paquin 151
Le Paradis Latin, Paris 115, 133
Les Parents Terribles 107
Patiño, Beatriz 83, 128
Perón, Eva 13, 25, 119
Petrushka 106, 107
Piège de Lumière 102, 107
Piguet, Robert *32*, 42, 44, *44*, *45*, 55, *73*, 103, 104, *150*, 151, 153
Pompidou, Claude 13, 128, *130*

Ré, Lorenzo 9, 56, 89
Rebaté, Lucienne 26
Reboux, Caroline 11, 21, 26; house of 83
Renaud, Madeleine 44, 103, 112
Reynaud, Paul 31
Ribes, Vicomtesse Jacqueline de 128, *129*
Ricci, Robert 51
Rivière, Catherine 11, 133
Rivière, Jean-Marie 115, 133
Rizzo, Willy *45*, *118*
Rochas, Marcel 42
Rothschild, Baroness Marie-Hélène de 128, 141
Ruggieri, Eve 70

Saint-Cyr, Claude 26
Saint-Cyr, Renée *89*
Saks Fifth Avenue, New York *96*, 100, *101*
Scherrer, Jean-Louis *153*, 153–54
Schiaparelli, Elsa 26
Shrimpton, Jean *136*
Simon, Pierre *94*
Snow, Carmel 75, 76, 79
Snowdon, Earl of (Antony Armstrong-Jones) *129*
Soraya of Iran, Princess 120, *123*
Suzy, Madame 26, 63, 97–98, 119
Svend 11
Swanson, Gloria 13, 119, *121*

'Théâtre de la Mode' *48–49*, *50*, 51, 55
Théâtre de l'Atelier, Paris 222
Théâtre de l'Athénée, Paris 104
Théâtre Marigny, Paris 103–4, 107
Théâtre le Palace, Paris 22, 115
Touchagues, Louis *50*, 51

Ungaro, Emanuel 151

Vivier, Roger 44, 103, 133
Vogue 13, 31, 41, 55, 103, 109

Windsor, Duchess of 13, *132*, 133